Rev Antu Mairie

signature
Nov 2009

How to Survive
The Apprentice!

Matthew Quinn

authorHOUSE®

AuthorHouse™ UK Ltd.
500 Avebury Boulevard
Central Milton Keynes, MK9 2BE
www.authorhouse.co.uk
Phone: 08001974150

© 2009 Matthew Quinn. All rights reserved.

No part of this book may be reproduced, stored in a retrieval system, or transmitted by any means without the written permission of the author.

First published by AuthorHouse 10/21/2009

ISBN: 978-1-4490-1798-9 (sc)

ISBN: 978-1-4490-1798-9 (sc)

This book is printed on acid-free paper.

Preface

The author has compiled this work whilst watching a heavily edited reality TV show. The opinions formed are those formed whilst under the influence of the editors and form only opinion. No offence is intended at the individuals named due to the characteristics shown by editors.

Contents

Preface	v
Introduction	ix
Chapter 1	1
"You're on show, not just on the show!"	
Chapter 2	7
"It's all about cleaning!"	
Chapter 3	21
"Hungry for business"	
Chapter 4	31
"Fit for business?"	
Chapter 5	44
"Leadership potential?"	
Chapter Six	53
"Commercial Sense – good or pants?"	
Chapter Seven	64
"The devil's in the detail"	
Chapter Eight	72
"Your order book is empty…"	
Chapter Nine	83
"Jolly boy's outing?"	

Chapter Ten	88
"Like taking candy….?"	
Chapter Eleven	98
"A real shot at TV stardom…?"	
Chapter Twelve	105
"Interview, or interrogation?"	
Chapter Thirteen	113
"A worthy winner?"	
Chapter Fourteen	117
"So what?"	
Acknowledgements	121
About the Author	123

Introduction

I love The Apprentice. In fact, it is the only reality TV show I watch. The other shows of the same genre have little appeal to me, because none of them give me what I love about The Apprentice.

Firstly, each week has a moral, as well as a learning point. You can watch the task and scream at the inefficiencies you see, as well as clucking your tongue at the terrible scenes in the boardroom.

Secondly, the central characters, i.e. Sir Alan, Nick, Margaret and the interviewers (the candidates are far from central in this show), know exactly what they are doing and play the foolishness of the candidates. There is nothing more gratifying than seeing a liar, or a fool get his comeuppance, and they do it well.

Thirdly, I have some admiration for Sir Alan and how he runs his empire – this may not be what you think it is, as I am not as sycophantic as some of the candidates, but I know a smart boy when I see one.

However, finally, and possibly the most important for a TV show, is the simple entertainment factor. Nowhere, in any media, do you get such a group of deluded fools, trying their best to look like serial entrepreneurs. If they were such a thing, why would they want a job that only paid them £100,000 pa? These days, that is not a real target for the best business brains in the country.

You too must love the show – I know this because you've picked up this book. Not because I have written it, you don't know me, this is my first book and we have probably never met. However, the title has attracted you. Therefore, I can deduce you have one of two reasons for reading it. One, you are thinking of applying to appear on the show, or two, you know there are business lessons to be learned from the show. The good news for you is that both of these objectives are covered in the pages of this book, along with some of my own observations, and with luck, a little bit of Apprentice type entertainment thrown in. I hope you will like it.

Allow me, at this point, to introduce myself. I have been a business consultant, salesperson and leader for a number of years, in various guises. I was one of the youngest people ever to win a place at the Royal Military Academy Sandhurst and, after leaving military service, I went on to sell cars for a large dealer group. I rose through the ranks, past sales manager and into the business manager role, ending up as business manager for Mercedes Benz on Park Lane, at the age of 27. I followed this with an account manager role and a management consultant role, operating as a global account manager across a wide range of industries, from entertainment, to media, oil, printing, logistics, finance and even genetic modification of pork meat. Finally, I came to rest as Head of Business Development for a top 10 financial services firm. I live in the countryside outside Edinburgh (in a house, I'm not a rabbit) with my wife Wendy and enjoy motorcycles, hiking, athletics, fishing, shooting, climbing, scuba diving and cooking. I am also an ambassador for the charity, John Thornton Young Achiever's Foundation, set up in memory of John, a Royal Marines Commando Officer killed in action in 2008. I love life and the best advice I ever got was to work to live, not live to work – I follow this and my friends will back me up on that.

Enough about me, let's look at Sir Alan himself, the anti – hero of our tale. One thing you must bear in mind about Sir Alan Sugar is that though he may be gruff, a megalomaniac, short and impolite, he is nobody's fool. This man has managed to get himself the opportunity of 18 hours (including the "You're Fired" show) of prime time TV coverage for his business. Further to this, a huge amount of newspaper time and people discussing him (as well as writing books) for a measly salary payment of £100,000 per annum – he gets to choose to whom this goes, from a cast of hopefuls and if he does not like them after a year, they disappear. At the time of writing this, 2 of the 4 winners no longer work for him and it seems a third is on his way out. Be under no illusions, Sir Alan is NOT looking for an Apprentice, if he was, he would not go to the TV. He is looking for coverage for his business and he has it. I like that about him. If you go on the show and win, always remember this – you are there for a year, if you do OK, you may stay, if not, you're fired!

One other note – to the person who bottled out of this year's show before the start – shame on you! You have taken another person's place and I hope that your mates, if you have any, are making fun of you right now for being soft!

Finally in this introduction, how to use the book. Read it from cover to cover. Then get the DVD of series 5 of The Apprentice and see what I mean. Then read it again. If you are looking for business lessons, use what you see and read and constantly evolve. If you are looking for the way to win the show, use these lessons in business and in the boardroom. Most important, get the DVD sets of ALL The Apprentice series and watch them again and again with these chapters in mind and you will see how easy it is to fail, but how much easier, and more fun it is to succeed!!!

All the way through this book, I want you to remember one thing – the definition of selling. This describes selling in it's optimum form and will be elaborated on chapter after chapter in this book.

Before you read mine – write your own down, think of a small child asking you what selling means. Then read the one below.

The best way to view selling is as a **buying process**, which the salesperson brings about in the customer

It **begins** with a **discovery** of **needs** to be met by the product being bought

It should be **enjoyable** to **both** parties

Chapter 1

"You're on show, not just on the show!"

Go and get a mirror, dress in your business attire and take a look at yourself.

The worst thing you can do in a business interview is look like you are trying to win a fashion show. The most successful person, by winning team standards in series 3 was a man called Paul Tulip. That guy could sell, he knew how to negotiate and was charming. As soon as the interview panel saw his shiny suit – he was doomed! This is real, people. Everyone makes a first impression as soon as they see you. A friend of mine, Mark Jeffries has written a great book called "What's Up With Your Handshake?". Buy it, read it, do it. I will paraphrase here from Mark, but not steal his thunder.

Now, you're looking in the mirror – smile. Extend your hand as if you shake with someone – freeze. What do you look like? If it is a footballer, a rock star, a person with a crooked arm, someone with a grimace, a scared person or a fool, then you are in the wrong. The best advice I ever heard on dressing and deportment was when I was in the army – my boss said, if you ever wear something or stand in a way that in 10 years time will look silly on a photograph – change! He was dead right.

Men – the rules!

- NO brown shoes for business, EVER!
- A tie should be the size of your thumb at the knot, the length of your thumb at it's widest and the width of your thumb from your trouser top.
- Your tie should not be plain, nor colourful – you cannot go wrong with wide stripes on a tie, but ensure they are British (high on the right as you look at it) not American (reverse).
- DO NOT wear a belt with your suit trouser – this tells me that it is not bespoke and does not fit, equally, do not have belt loops – why are they there without a belt?
- Jacket should come to below your trouser front pocket and should have at least one, preferably two vents in the back.
- Suits are dark, not shiny and if you have a pinstripe, make it subtle.
- Pockets are your own style, but never put anything in the pockets of any suit, apart from a slim wallet in the inside jacket and a folded handkerchief in the trouser.
- Single breasted suits are better for business, simply because you can wear them open, or buttoned. The number of buttons should never be more than three, no more than one should ever be buttoned and the bottom one is only there to help the jacket hang, so do not use it.
- Jacket cuffs should have buttons, and they should work.
- Avoid fashion, as a classic suit will always look better.
- Lining can be brightly coloured, because only you should see it.
- Shirts should be light coloured, patterned with lines if you want, never short sleeved, never with a chest

- pocket (what's that for?) never black or brown, always double cuffs, with sober cufflinks and long enough to show half an inch of cuff beyond your suit.
- Shoes should be black, leather soled and highly polished – never patent leather or rubber soles. It is your choice as to loafers or laces, but please, do not buy pointed toes!
- If you wear a tie, wear it properly, no top button undone and tie sagging. If you want to open your collar – remove your tie completely.
- Jewellery should be restricted to a nice watch (no 'bling') a Rolex submariner is always best, followed by an Omega Seamaster and if you must, third, a Tag.
- SHAVE! For heavens' sake, shave.
- Hair should be neat, combed and clean.
- Spend money on a good tailor. Tony Stein from Norton and Townsend will give you a good deal if you mention my name. He is so good, he makes me look great and believe me, at 6 feet 7 and 17 stone, I need all the help I can get!
    - I take it I do not have to mention comedy ties, cartoon socks and "hilarious" cufflinks?

Women – the rules!

- Not too much make up
- Do not have anything (hair or jewellery) that gets in the way or that you have to constantly mess with
- No floaty scarves or dresses, you are at a job interview, not Ascot
- No long splits up the skirt that you have to close every time you sit down
- High heels are fine, high soles are not, you will look like a stripper

- Treat your colour choices in the same way as the men do – nothing too bright, or sparkly, sober and tidy is the best way
- Avoid trendy and stay with classic
- Do not 'power' dress – it looks ridiculous and men do not believe it anyway
- If you cannot operate machinery with the nails you have – they are too long
- Choose a look and stick with it – please, no Lucinda Burger type hats, colours or wackiness, everyone hates wacky!
- Hair should be clean and not styled in a way which takes an hour to sort in the morning, people will lose patience with you in a shared house

All, if you are fat or unhealthy, lose weight and get fit before you start, try "Fighting Fit" by Adrian Weale. Bad health and obesity make people think of useless, lazy people, not my fault, just a fact!

What NOT to say.

In your interviews, remember, whatever stupid thing you say (and you will say something stupid) Adrian Chiles and the newspapers will dive on it, making you a laughing stock until the day you lose and then ignoring you thereafter. Some examples –

- I would say I was the best salesperson in Europe!
    - Eh? Where is the proof? Why only Europe?
- The spoken word is my tool!
    - Surely, this should be; My tool is the spoken word…. If you cannot get the grammar right, forget it
- I am just a serial entrepreneur

- - In that case, Sir Alan will not want you, he needs a person with some commitment
- Making money is better than sex!
  - Son, you're doing it wrong, or you're doing it with the wrong person!

You get my drift. Be confident, but ensure you have your "30 second pitch" ready. Straplines are pointless, they will not win you the show and they will not endear you to the audience, however, like in any business arena, you must be ready when someone asks "What do you do?" Watch the scenes in the car in episode one and decide how you can say – "This is who I am, this is what I do, this is why I'm successful at it, this is 1 strength, this is 1 weakness and this is why I'm here." In less than a minute though please.

Finally – if you shake hands with someone, please stand up! I know that traditionally women don't have to, however, in business there is no gender. It is completely unforgiveable for a man to shake hands sitting down. Introduce yourselves before you get in the cars.

Use these first few days as a networking opportunity. You will be in battle with the rest of the people soon enough, but for now, relish the fact that, if nothing else, you are with like minded people, as well as the fact that you have made it to the show. Celebrate that, look like you are about to enjoy yourself and be friendly. These people could be good contacts after the show for many reasons, so don't use the time to scope out the competition and plan how you are going to be ruthless – it does not make any sense and everyone, I mean everyone, is watching. Use some basic networking rules –

- Smile
- Plan your 'route of introductions'
- Speak to people for a while and find a way to move on

- – you have lots of people to meet
- Do not be random or vague
- Remember names – repeat them to yourself if need be, but don't look like you are using the old, tired trick of "Using the client's name" – some fools even do this in emails these days, which is just creepy
- Give some information about yourself, but do not bore or boast, remember your "30 second pitch"
- Be aware of your presence
- Most important of all – BE INTERESTED, NOT INTERESTING. It will get you a lot further!

Lastly, go into this game with an objective – not "To be the next apprentice." You only, at this point have a one in 16 chance of that. Also don't be soft, avoid "I hope not to get fired in the first show." If you think that, you probably will be.

Set yourself 3 objectives, your must, intend and like.

I MUST get to know who in my team fits the profiles of "seller", "buyer", "negotiator", "planner", "do – er", "budgeter" and "challenger", in order to use them when I am team leader.

I INTEND to lead the task which is based around sales (there always is one) as sales management is my skill and I will give myself the best chance of winning it.

I'd LIKE to portray myself as a good listener in a team, a challenging adviser and a good leader, because that is what Sir Alan is looking for.

If you feel really comfortable, be the leader in the first task – if you lose, you have a high chance of being fired, but if you win, you have set a standard, but it takes balls of steel. To give you a hint – I'd do it!

Chapter 2

"It's all about cleaning!"

It's not you know.

Sir Alan introduces the task, each week with a statement like this, he also gives the teams a brief to read. It is totally staggering to me how few people actually read the brief. This is exactly why Sir Alan does this – he wants to see who thinks that the task is "All about cleaning"!

In business it is exactly the same – it is very easy, in a meeting to start at a point ambiguous to the task in hand, if one is not totally clear on an objective and that objective has been challenged for clarity, all can be undone! No matter how hard you work. This is why this first week is a great one, sometimes my favourite – not only do we get to meet the cast of characters for the first time, but we see who actually has the sense to see through the complex and into the simple. Every year, during this show, we hear the narrator saying –

"Sir Alan Sugar left school at 16 and sold car aerials from the back of a van!"

Many people are agog with amazement about this – wow! An £800mm empire from a van with car aerials. If it were that easy, why does everyone not do it? The reason is, simplicity

– Sir Alan was never going to make a career from car aerials, what he needed was start up capital, so he bought something, and sold it for more. He knew his objective and he saw a way to do it. There are people out there, the same age as Sir Alan, still selling car aerials from the back of a van – they don't have a private jet!

Every time this task is set, just like with the fish market last year, Sir Alan makes the mental calculation, spend, sell, profit – you must do the same to win, in the task, as well as in business.

Therefore this task is not about cleaning, or fish, or whatever. It is all about profit!

Here is what to remember – spend little, sell lots. Forget everything else for now, I don't care how good a business prospect you are, one year some crazy person was trying to convince customers that they needed a 24 hour helpline service for laundry, one woman wanted a certain type of picture placed on the top of each cup of coffee. Now is not the time for initiative, Sir Alan is looking for –

- Minimal Spend
- Customer Knowledge
- Hard Work

And most of all –

- A Plan

Howard, the boys' team leader this year said "What is our objective?" He was mocked by his peers, however, what a great question to ask – although as a leader in this task, he would have been better off saying –

"Fellers, our objective today is to make as much profit as possible in a day whilst spending as little as possible on the initial outlay!"

It sounds dictatorial, but so what – the first task is there to get things going and you need to move fast – every action you take on that first day can be sanity checked back to that objective, imagine if the girls had done that whilst spending their £196.45 on materials..... where does that fit in the "little as possible on the initial outlay"? it doesn't, and believe me, real business is no different!

If we take the cleaning task as an example which can build a process –

- Set the objective
- Decide what you need to buy (and please don't buy something you cannot use, or don't understand – like a jetwasher!)
- Look at how much you then have to spend, and challenge this
- Get some market knowledge
- Decide on who has the sales skills
- Get going!!!

Oh, hold on a moment, this was an example around the recent cleaning task – but it seems to work for the fish task last year, as well as the first task the year before and…business itself – funny that!

What to buy?

How would you decide on what to buy – well the task is all important here, as is the knowledge of to whom you are selling. Straight away I would have a question – are we selling to customers (the man on the street) or to business? Simplicity says that both these avenues will work, but for different reasons and in different ways, however, it is a big mistake to be vague about the two. It would also strike me that this is a good way to split the teams, if you have to. Choose the team members on the basis of their experience, business or customer. If you have a car salesman in the ranks, they will be far better employed talking to a man in the street than a multinational business director in his office. This is not me being rude, as a "Global Account Director" would be equally useless the other way around – know your strengths and that of your team!

If you are going to wash cars in a supermarket car park whilst people shop, you only need a bucket, sponge and soap – if you left your car with a stranger in Tesco car park whilst you wandered for an hour, would you lock it? Of course you would – this means that not only can you not clean the inside, but also the customer does not want you to – so don't buy a vacuum cleaner – get it?

If you are planning to clean classic cars on a forecourt, buy the best looking materials you can – the owners of these cars are notoriously proud, so be proud with them.

Spend, therefore, as little as you can. As soon as you have decided what to buy – look at it again for 2 minutes (time well spent) and quickly say to yourself – "Do I really need that?"

Market Knowledge

Here is where some leadership and planning come in. Now you need some market knowledge – none of the teams this year had any of this, the team last year, selling fish, thought they had it but didn't and anyone who overcomplicates this, or indeed forgets it is a fool!

If you are in the team dedicated to the man on the street and are cleaning cars – ask yourself some questions.

- Where would you be where you could happily leave your car for a little while during the day?

- At work
- At the supermarket
- At home
  - During the day, the above ideas are probably populated in that order – therefore I would head to an industrial estate and knock some doors down. Once I had been to every single business on it, I would go to another. When I ran out of industrial estates, I would go to a supermarket, one without a built in car wash – you don't want to argue with a store manager, you don't have time. I would ask the store manager for a pitch, pay him if need be, or at the very least hand him a nice bottle after the day and stand at the doorway asking everyone who came in if they want their car washing!

- What would you want from a car clean?
  - As I have pointed out, the car is locked, so I want the outside to be clean – I would pay more for a polish, but a wash is all I need right now.
- How long should it take?
  - If it were me, and I were in my office with no need to leave, I would not care – but it would be good for the washer to ask when I needed my car. If I were in the supermarket and I would be shopping for 30 minutes, if you still had not finished my car by the time I come out, I would drive off, soap flying everywhere and no cash in your hand! Don't hold me up, I want to leave the supermarket as soon as possible!
- How much would I pay?

- For a car clean? No more than a tenner, but more likely a fiver. Nothing in between, because I neither have, nor want, change! If I am at work I have only notes, if I am at the supermarket I have paid with my card so have notes only, and I am more likely to agree to spend on the way in, so don't ask me when I'm coming out!

It all seems so simple when I put it like that – however when one over complicates it, bad things happen. Remember – you are a customer of somebody – you know the answers to these questions, whether you have a degree in global marketing or not – become a human for a while and look at what you would want from this!

If you are on the team who is approaching businesses, think a little. Ensure that your skills are being used well, if you do not like cold calling, don't volunteer to do it, equally, if you are the leader, don't choose the most monotone person to make those calls – find a bulldog. Open the yellow pages and get 2 people making calls to make an appointment with your customer – however, they should remember at this point that they are not selling the car wash – they are selling the appointment. It is EXACTLY the same in business, know what you are selling and base your call around that, people who blab on about their product will lose the attention.

Remember the elevator speech! Ignore anyone who tells you that an elevator speech is designed to let people know what you are selling, in a short space of time – it is not designed to do this at all. An elevator speech is designed to *get you an appointment* to tell people what you are selling – there is a huge difference!

"Hi, my name is Matthew from Gleamy gleam car valeting. We make your forecourt shine by polishing your stock to the best it can be!"

"We have standard rates for vehicles such as yours and I would like to get a time in your diary this morning to come down and do you a good job!"

You will always be asked "How much do you charge?", whether it is on the phone, or in person. Rule one in this situation is this – if you are asked a direct question, give a direct answer. If I ask you what your price is, I expect you to know. If you stammer, think, pontificate or tell me that it 'depends', you will be out of my office so fast you'll bounce a foot high from the pavement on your head – seriously.

So, I hear you cry! How can we know what our price is? Simple, when some of your team are making calls for appointments, use another person to call the real Gleamy gleam car valeting and ask how much they will charge you for your 3 classic cars, as well as what they do and how long it takes. In fact, if your appointment team does really well and you have more business than you can handle, you can farm the overflow out to Gleamy gleam for a finders fee of £50 – easy money, doing nothing!

When in front of a customer, remember, the first rule of announcing a price is "He who bids first wins!" – but only when you have done the research around your other customers – Jasmina almost proved this when in the Stretch Humvee rental office, although she did come in at a mad price of £300 a car which they had 'worked out'. How had they 'worked it out'? They sat in the car and did some sums for ages, until they found a price, around which they had guessed and quickly realised that they were wrong – the foolish.

I would have picked up the phone, whilst sitting outside the Humvee office and described the cars to a competitor to find out what they did and for how much, then done the sums to check I could afford it (although I would have spent less in the first place) and wandered in with an extra tenner on their price. Simple, quick, effective, just what Sir Alan is looking for and just what your current boss is looking for.

Finally, follow up on your promise – this is not a long standing business, so don't worry about recommendations and customer service..... but you need to do it right. The boys spent an hour cleaning a car, only to be told, as well as shown, that it was sub standard – not acceptable, in fact I'm surprised that they were even allowed near the others – we all know how to clean a car, just get on with it.

Let's look at some of the blinding mistakes made, both in the business world as well as the TV show.

- Don't overspend
- Make a plan
- Don't argue with the customer, as Mona did – if he says it's £40 a car and you have not done your market research, he is right. Only debate it if you know your facts
- Don't hold out your hand asking to shake on a deal – I would throw you out of my office for that one – after wasting as much of your time as possible so you lost, of course
- Don't be a negative influence on the team, either as a team leader, or member – it does nobody any good at all
- Don't miss opportunities – the kerbside car clean was a long time coming in the girls team
- Do the job right first time – this task is simple, make it so
- Deliver your promise, but make sure you have promised the right thing in the first instance
- Don't lose cash – Debra's car cleaning team lost £100 – by that I mean it was there for the taking and it slipped them by because the job was bad
- Don't go for low income answers – shoe shining in a shopping centre – no thanks!

- Figure out what the agreed result is first and follow it – don't spend an hour washing a car only to find out the customer is not happy – ask the inspector what he will be looking for first, and do it
- As a leader, step back ever so often to check what is going on – don't lose the wood for the trees – everyone knows you can clean a car, that's not your job here – lead, don't just 'do'!
- Assign a quality control man to check your work before the customer sees it
- Set that objective and check everything against it!

All these rules slip straight into real business – the life of a successful business these days is simple – as soon as you overcomplicate it, you will struggle. This first task is a great set of lessons for people who are entrepreneurs and need some quick start up capital, or people with a product to sell and limited funds to use. Remember, you are a customer of somebody, ask yourself what you would want, what you would do and how much you would pay and you will not go far wrong.

If you are the leader in the first task, here is what to do to win and subsequently send the other team into the boardroom.

- Set an objective – make sure it is a good one "Make lots of money and beat the other team" is for saps
- Make a plan which fits your objective
- Know your team – assign roles to fit each person's skills
- Ensure that each person's brief is clear and that they have relevant authority
- Communicate, constantly
- Get the market, or customer knowledge

- Control and update
- Occasionally, step back and look, from a different angle at your team. Remember, there are a couple of million people screaming at their TV screen right now, but only because they can see the bigger picture
- Give good feedback – ensure people know when they are doing well, or badly
- Crush uprisings positively
- Keep a motivational and positive outlook
- Stay consistent
- Show some integrity, it, if nothing else will help you forever in business and will certainly save you in the boardroom

If you are a team member and want your team to do well, or ultimately stay out of the boardroom, remember –

- Offer your skills
- Do the job assigned to you, whether you like it or not, it is not for life, for heavens' sake
- Think about what your customer wants and what your customer needs
- Challenge the leader in a positive and appropriate way – think of Ruth Badger at the beginning of the show 2 years ago and do the opposite
- Deliver your promise
- Support the leader
- Show integrity, if you have something to say, say it to the right person and stand by it
- This is not the time to 'play the game' – that is for the boardroom

These rules will help in business, as well as in The Apprentice.

More important, they will keep you out of the boardroom if your team loses!

In short – week 1, profit counts for everything – do not overspend.

Boardroom Tactics

There are 3 elements to the boardroom conversations –

1. Where both teams are present
2. When the losing team is present
3. Where the three people in the firing line are present

These elements each have a different objective

1. Don't be seen
2. Don't be chosen
3. Don't be fired

Forget everything else at this point. this is where you play the game with all your might, remember, you are fighting on 2 fronts. First is to win the game. However, believe me, by this point Sir Alan knows who his final 5 players are, if it is not you, then you cannot win. Second is to make good TV – if you make good TV then you will stay longer.

When both teams are present in the boardroom, whatever you say does not matter. There is a simple reason for this – if your team have won, you won't get fired, so what is the point of speaking up and ruffling feathers, particularly those of Sir Alan. You will make no friends and only do yourself harm. Therefore until you know which team has won or lost – shut up. Unless of course there has been a question directed straight at you, in which case answer, politely, briefly and efficiently.

If you have been unlucky enough to find yourself on the losing team, play the game for all you are worth.

In order not to be chosen –

- Be brief and succinct if asked a question
- Be honest
- Ensure what you are saying is in line with your actions during the task – you do not want to surprise or annoy the team leader right now as they will just choose you to be in the firing line
- Sit up straight – Sir Alan needs his daily dose of worship
- Never waffle or pull faces, it just annoys the man in charge
- Never say "some people" or "others" – great business people are ALWAYS specific, if you must give an example, use names and facts – if nothing else, you are more likely to be believed
- If you give an example, be clear on the facts, the result and what your point is
- If you are giving an opinion, say "I firmly believe…." Not "I think…." People will follow you more readily
- If you want to play the game, support the leader, but only if it goes along with your actions through the task
- Always call Sir Alan "Sir Alan" – stay on his side as he values courtesy

Finally, and always, have an answer to the two most common questions asked in the boardroom –

"Why should I not fire you?"

"What will you bring to my party?"

If you cannot answer these, succinctly and clearly, you deserve to be fired.

If you are unlucky enough to be brought into the boardroom to be in the firing line, you have 2 options –

Fight, or Quiet?

Don't try to do both – this year Mona was very nearly fired by trying to do a little bit of both, and Anita was forgotten about until she spoke up and decided to accept responsibility for everything ("Can I put my own case forward?"). One thing – don't pull faces or be dramatic – this will annoy Sir Alan and give Adrian Chiles an easy job on his show.

Fighting makes better TV, so you have a good chance of staying, there have been many examples of this – Jo the brummie girl was an absolute disaster, but made it through the boardroom on a number of occasions by shouting and crying. Kate the blonde posh girl was the same, only flirting and fighting rather than crying and finally Ruth Badger, the queen of all boardroom fighters and has since made a career from being a bit shouty and opinionated. So it must work!

If you decide to fight –

- Give clear examples of why the others deserve to go
- Choose a victim and attack, don't fight on 2 fronts – it didn't work for Napoleon and it won't work for you
- Never admit any mistake
- Be succinct
- Avoid fillers ("At the end of the day" etc)
- Before you speak – think!

If you decide to be quiet, which nearly worked for Anita –

- Don't dig a hole by speaking
- Answer only questions directed at you
- Claim to be quiet through disbelief if asked
- Defend yourself against specific points against you, but refuse to be drawn into speculation about others or that about which you have no knowledge
- Don't laugh, be sarcastic, or rude

Week One – the result!

There were three people in the boardroom in week one.

Anita, Debra and Mona. The simple fact is that nobody in their right mind would employ any of these three, ever. Debra is horrid, rude and arrogant, Mona is rambling and emotional and Anita is vacuous. Sir Alan knows this, so he is not looking to give any of these people a chance to be his apprentice. Therefore it stands that he is looking to keep the people who will make the best TV in order to keep people watching.

Mona is exotic, coming from Tanzania, as well as good looking. Add to this that it is always funny to watch a face pulling cry baby on TV and she was safe for another few weeks.

Debra was vicious, spiteful and full of lies and hate. She also had a good amount of smirking looks which draws one to loathe her immediately, making her safe, in my guess (this is being written at the time of the show), until at least week 8.

Anita, I'm sorry, but I've forgotten you already and it is only the morning after the show aired! She claims to have been one of the best business prospects in Britain, is a lawyer and has high intelligence – we saw none of it, she would not make good TV, therefore – YOU'RE FIRED.

Week one – the right choice, well done Sir Alan.

Chapter 3

"Hungry for business"

This week Sir Alan gave a clever spin on his task and not many people noticed it. The spin was that he had set 2 separate tasks and the way to smash this one is to treat it as that. This happens all the time in business – people start on a job, a project or an agreement and don't slice the tasks up to their relevant aspects. Not only is it a guiding time management principle to do this, but also good business sense. Look into this more deeply.

Anyone who is in FMCG (fast moving consumer goods) can learn a lot from this week.

The task this week was to set up a catering service. Straight away you have an overall guide – the prominent word here, if it were real life, is SERVICE. If this were a real business, service is what would get you the success. However, this is not a real business, no matter how many times the girls answer the phone as "Ignite catering." Or refer to their project manager as the "CEO". The task in hand here is to make as much money as possible, which means that the guiding principles from the last chapter still apply – spend less, make more.

However, the first thing to do is split your focus – one to look after task 1 (lunch) and one to look after task 2 (evening reception). You cannot succeed in this task without doing this, as if the two areas become embroiled, you will end up losing, as the boys proved.

Both the teams started, not by splitting the tasks, but by deciding on a theme – Jasmina, the girls leader told us that the most important management skill we can have is to "cut the crap". I'm not sure which book she has been reading, as the first few hours of her team leading were full of crap, although she did redeem herself later. The least professional part of her planning was the confident target of making a 70% profit margin – she then came in with almost 300%. If one of my managers forecasted and then was 230% out – in either direction – I'd be concerned. Forecasting is a skill and should be treated as such. Planning on 70% margin and then bringing in 4 times that smacks of pure luck, and I'm afraid that luck does not work in long term business. Although, it saved Jasmina from the boardroom, so fair play to her.

Rocky had a lot to prove – he owns a chain of sandwich shops so had to be the team leader. If he had not come forward and they had lost, he would certainly have been fired, for not using his skills. Therefore there was no question that the choice of leader was right, from Rocky's point of view. However, he was led astray by the others and that is where his downfall was.

If you decide on a theme – use it! I cannot have been the only one to notice that whilst the girls' theme was 'Italian' (good choice, easy to make and cheap) the boys' theme started off as '2012 Olympics' and morphed somehow into '5 continents, with some togas and shorts'. This makes no sense – if the theme is the Olympics, forget the 5 continents, that is a theme of 'foreign lands'. An Olympic theme has 'Pincent's Pancetta' and 'Boxer's Baguette' with sports themed nutritional ingredients. I guarantee that in business, if you get an idea and allow someone to alter it, not in process but in intent, the way will be lost. This is what happened to the boys.

However, criminally, for both teams, I could not see from what they were doing, whether their focus was on lunch, or the evening reception. Why have a theme for lunch? I have worked in the City, customers want you to just give them some food that is easy to eat and a drink and get out of their way.

The first customer contact in this task was to get some lunch orders – this was a catalogue of business disasters, although the girls had made a good stab at planning what to make.

First, and again, you will start to see how important it is, focus on the two tasks – forget your Olympic theme for lunch, nobody cares, ask the customer what they want and make it for them. If you came to me with an Olympic themed lunch I would worry about how long my team were spending eating it. If you asked me what I wanted I would respond –

"Small sandwiches with easy fillings, fruit, crisps and a cake to finish – don't worry about too much garnish, but I have 15% of my staff who are vegetarians." Now, I know nothing about catering, as do most of your clients, but I do know what my team and I want for lunch. All you need to do now is price it up and deliver it. This was the second mistake – giving the Olympic lunch pitch and allowing the customer to call you back later. Get the information, leave, price it up and then you call them back, give a price and get a decision. This works for any Fast Moving Consumer Goods service offering, it's basic!

The girls had a more basic lunch offering, with a set price and it worked – I am not sure it would have worked in real life, without the weight of Sir Alan and a TV camera behind it, but it did for the task. I would guarantee that there would be no repeat orders though.....

The boys had no lunch orders, so sold on the streets – they found a gold mine at the south bank and then went back once everything was sold – or at least one team did. If you find a goldmine, tell your team mates – this could have saved them at least the embarrassment of a loss!!

In pitching for the evening function, as in any business, there are rules to follow –

- Please – put someone in the room who has experience – Jasmina was criminally negligent in putting her team in to pitch. She is the expert, she should be there
- Find out what the customer wants – the business conversation should always go before the features and benefits presentation, all great salespeople know that and all great salespeople do that in every customer meeting
- Do the research, but know what you are researching, Howard rang someone in catering, but was talking about a completely different offering – I'm sure that the people to whom he spoke were not dressed in togas. Also, if you do the research, you do the pitch – then at least you can compare like for like.
- Get your pricing right before you go in – for a couple of seconds, I actually felt sorry for the odious Philip – he was told to pitch at £60, and did so, good for him. However, he did not know what that price was for, what the customer wanted or what he could go down to before having to change the offer. Big mistake.

Luckily, I then stopped feeling sorry for him, as there is no excuse for poor negotiation, it is the easiest part of business, as well as the most fun! Clearly he had done no business conversation either.

- He who bids first wins! But only if you have all the detail. Philip put a price of £65 a head on the table. All the customer said was – "I'm not impressed!" and the price was slashed – where is the sense in that?
- If a customer tells you that your first bid is too expensive, you must know whether it is over budget, or under value. Otherwise you cannot move on – the only, one, primary, possible way to find this out is to ask – and the

magic questions is as follows – "IS THAT OVER YOUR BUDGET, OR DO YOU NOT SEE THE VALUE". Write that down gang! It is a lifesaver.

- If the answer is given that it is over budget, then you can ask – "What is your budget and what would you want included?"
- If the answer is that they do not see the value, you can ask – "So you have the budget then?" and find out what would increase the value (I can bet it would be to get rid of the togas in this case…..)
- If you need to work things out, or call the boss, have a time out, leave the room and discuss things – this is allowed you know.
- Please, never, ever work things out in a meeting with a calculator – if you did that with me, I would ask how you came to your price, if you cannot answer, you're out of the door as the calculator is clearly for show.
- If you give a concession on price, take one on service too. If your price is 90% lower by the end but your service is the same, I will be very worried indeed about your integrity.

However, in the case of this show, here is what happened –

Philip gave an outrageous price. The lady said that this price was more for a sit down meal (there is a hint here – what would you like included…). The man said "I'm not impressed." Magically, 45% of the price disappeared – I must try this next time I buy a car….. Luckily for us though, Philip said "Let's get realistic!". OK, let's get realistic, get out of my office.

The 'realistic' price was £35 a head – a full 45% discount from a moment ago – the man must have seen how well he was doing, as he simply repeated himself – "I'm not impressed!". Philip (working something out on a calculator, but nobody, including his 2 stooges, knows what) tells us that it would be "Incredibly realistic" (there's a lot of realism here) to ask for £17.50. Bear in mind that this is for EXACTLY the same service.

Our man now knows he is on to a winner, as he just, once more, repeats himself; "I'm not impressed!". More jabs on the calculator from our Phil and bang! We are now at £15 a head – for the same thing! Luckily for Philip, this gets agreed – containing the loss Rocky suffers to a mere couple of hundred quid. Sir Alan called Philip a spiv in the boardroom and I could not agree more. All responsibility for this rests on his shoulders and I would have fired him anyway, just as I would anyone in my business that acted like that. Negotiation is an art, it is also a lot of fun and anyone who degrades it the way Philip did should be nowhere near any business. I understand he is an estate agent – beware – if you have him as your agent, you'd be better doing ALL the negotiations yourself. Although, you could probably get away with only paying a tiny fee through him though……

The next step is organisation. This was a most impressive feat from the girls and Jasmina in particular. Here she came into her own. This girl is not the best business woman in the world, but she can certainly manage a kitchen. She did 2 things very well –

1 – She had cost control. She learned this from the previous week, although cost control is not just buying the cheapest goods as she did. Be aware that in real life, cheap goods equals bad experience equals no further orders – did not matter here, but one to remember.

2 – She organised everyone to their skills in the kitchen. She also had everyone motivated and smiling and when the actual function came about, the motivation was still there and they came across as efficient and professional

Rocky did neither of these and so failed. If Jasmina had appointed some kind of quality controller, her role would have been perfect. She may have realised she did not need one to win the task and took a gamble at the inevitable fine from the customer, we will never know. If she did know this, then she has a chance to win the show.

Finally, in this performance is the evening function itself –

A good manager (rather than leader) is paramount here and Jasmina proved that over Rocky.

In The Apprentice, dressing up for a task is never a good idea – none of the dressing up attempts have ever impressed, although they do make good TV and allow Adrian Chiles an easy life. The reason that dressing up has never impressed is twofold. Firstly, it adds to your spend, if you try to save money on costumes, they look tacky, cue the boys in togas..... secondly, if the theme is not clear (again the theme has changed, from Olympics, to 5 continents (dressed as sportsmen) to ancient Greece (dressed in Roman togas.....) can you see how easily the message is diluted. If there was a theme of Olympics, deck the halls with posters of our medal winners, have Gold Medal fillings in the pies, dress in the Olympic off duty uniform of blazers and slacks and fly the Union Flag in the venue. This would entice excitement and conversation far more than 'dressing up' and would reduce the amount that your customer fines you for incompetence. Well dressed and professional, with a theme (which should always be clear, but just below the surface) will always overcome cheaply acquired costumes and having to tell people your theme. This rule applies for both business and The Apprentice.

Also, control of what you are promising is required – Jasmina shone through this as her girls were still buzzing from the kitchens and she had built their trust.

In summary –

- Ensure you see a task as 2 separate tasks if appropriate

- If you have a theme or idea – stick to the intent, but take feedback on the implementation
- Make the simple things simple – lunch is just lunch
- Negotiate with integrity and skill
- Control costs, not just by buying cheap goods, but by forecasting and understanding
- Be efficient in production
- Be professional in execution

Week two is about seeing the difference in the tasks and doing two things well.

If you want to win the game, buy cheap goods, if you want to win in business, work on your customer service.

Boardroom Tactics

If you lose money in this game – you are in a shaky seat from the start, therefore be very sure you are taking in the people responsible for the loss. If you get your boardroom fellows wrong – you're fired!

Remember, there are 3 stages to the boardroom, just as before –

- Stage one – everyone in there together
- Stage two – just the losing team
- Stage three – just the final three

Stage one tactics are always the same – keep your mouth shut until you know who has won or lost – this is not the time to be making enemies.

Stage two – as before but now with an added extra – At this point, listen, particularly if you are the leader, to what Nick and Margaret say. Remember, these two have been watching intensely for the whole of the task and will have seen far more than you. They will also be advising Sir Alan when you are not there, so hold an awful lot of weight. This point is proven this week when, during stage two, Nick, with a typical raise of the eyebrow, told Noorul that he had "made it his business to watch" him throughout the task. He had done this because he felt Noorul had done nothing. I cannot believe that Rocky missed this opportunity to play into their hands. The person that really talked himself into the chair was James. Remember, show no emotion in this stage, unless you want to make good TV. However, saying you are hurt, like when your cat died, is just weak.

The real choices for the boardroom were Noorul and Philip. Noorul because Nick had already got him marked and clearly disliked him and Philip because he was so dismal in the negotiation and therefore was directly responsible for the loss. Believe me, a monkey could survive this boardroom with those two in there. My guess would have been that it would be the end of Philip – but sadly, not.

Stage three – remember fight or quiet? James was being petulant, but again was making good TV, however, he nearly went when asked the question "who should I fire James?". If you are asked this, make a choice – James said "fire both of them" – that is clearly a cop out because, whilst James is quite, quite useless, Howard, in this task had no reason to be there, particularly as he had won the first task – he is still almost bombproof.

Week Two – the result!

Rocky's only defence here could be that if he had not become team leader, he would be being fired for cowardice and at least he stepped up with his experience. He was simply let down by negotiation and sales skills. If he had Philip in with him and had said that – goodbye Philip.

However, Philip and Noorul were not in the room. Rocky had the experience and should have managed the task better, Howard had no reason to be in the firing line and petulant James is making good TV. Therefore, Rocky – YOU'RE FIRED!

Week two – right choice, well done again Sir Alan!

Chapter 4

"Fit for business?"

The task this week was to design and sell a piece of home fitness equipment. This type of task always appears around this time in The Apprentice, because it is easy to get wrong, spectacularly. However, with the correct processes, it is also pretty easy to get it right, spectacularly.

The reason Sir Alan likes this kind of task is because his main businesses revolve around manufacturing, the telephones, computers and fax machines are all designed, marketed and sold in his empire. Therefore it is something with which he is familiar. The task also shows off some clear business skills and process management.

In essence, any manufacturing business should be split into three areas –

- Designing
- Marketing
- Selling

All the skills needed to perform well should be in your team somewhere. Creative types should be designing. The look, feel and use of the product should be looked after by marketers and the sales people should sell. Therefore the team should be split, from the start, into these areas.

The big issue in this task, as in many businesses is that the people lose focus on where they should be – the project manager should ensure that everyone is clear on their role and that is the role they should do. The easy thing to happen here is that the person (in this week's case, the increasingly irritating Ben) who has the most to do with the design ends up doing everything. Other people (the unfortunate Maj) then end up standing around doing nothing. Know your team – focus them on the task that they have and work towards the three goals – design, market and sell.

We will speak more about leadership later in the book, however, for now, we will concentrate on how a project like this is managed and the skills that each team requires.

When things like this task go wrong, it is always because of the grey area between the roles – for example, if design people try to market the product, they fail because being too emotionally close to the product blocks their objectivity. If marketing people try to sell a product they will fail as they repeatedly bash the way the product is made over people's heads rather than selling it. We'll talk about the 6 step sales process that all great salespeople use later, but for now, it's important to understand the cycle that everyone goes through EVERYTIME they buy ANYTHING.

- Need Awareness
    - I have a clammy mouth due to 20 pints, I need to clear it
    - My car is broken, I need to get to work
- Product awareness
    - Mints! That's what I need!
    - A new car! That's what I need!
- Provider awareness
    - Tesco across the road

- - Audi dealer in the yellow pages
- Deal Awareness
  - 37p for some polo mints? OK!
  - £1100 deposit and £500 a month over 4 years? OK!
- Comfort awareness
  - Mouth feels better!
  - Car drives nice!

No matter what you buy, EVER, you will do this – if it is a packet of polo mints then it will happen in 10 seconds, if it is a television it may take a week, a car may take a month, a house 6 months and so on. Equally, sooner or later, you'll go back to the start, making it a cycle.

The important thing here is to understand where your customer is in the process and who deals with each part.

Marketing people sort out the first three – they tell people what they need (push marketing) or they ask people what they want (pull marketing), then they tell people what will solve their problem and where to get it.

Sales people sort out the deal – with a 6 step sales process.

Customer service types look after the comfort.

If I were to split a team in a task like this, I would follow this pattern.

Design – go and see the personal trainers and gym people, find out what is out there, what is missing and what people use.

Marketing – go and see what sells, ask retailers what their profit margins are and what kind of numbers they sell on a monthly basis. Ask who their customers are and then go and ask the customer the same questions.

Sales – start talking to your retailers – ask what they see as a problem which your product can solve, find out what makes them buy and how much stock they hold.

Just as a break in proceedings here, to revert back to the actual show – can I suggest that Sir Alan should have fired Debra on the spot for her disgraceful racism when speaking to Jasmina. Positive discrimination is still discrimination and acting like a superhero when someone is making a valid point is awful – she should be out.

As soon as the teams did not split in this way – they started to fail…. You will see Ben try to both design and market their product. The product is HIS idea which means that he is too passionate about it to be objective – it is wonderful to have passion and to come alive when you see you idea take shape, however, James, the team leader, should have moved him well away from the marketing. Look for this in your business and you will see it everywhere – it does not have to be a manufactured product, but maybe just an idea – I know as I have been guilty of it and I see it every day in my business.

Another issue they faced was the structure of their process. They designed, then took photos and made marketing material and then they went out on the pitch. Both groups met their first customer and were told that they sold high end equipment for a few thousand pounds to their customers. Why were they even there in the first place – some even carried on with their sale – point your attention to your market. By the time the prototype was ready, you should have had your marketing team speaking to people as well as your sales team speaking to people – ready to design your 'pitch'.

The pitch itself is amazing – every time I see The Apprentice I am amazed at the fact that the WORST person possible is always asked to pitch. Remember the girl last year talking about the cat calendar? Lorraine this year was no better. I am always amazed at the lack of presentation skills in business as a whole these days. Bear in mind, I present for a living, so when I say this, it is considered. PowerPoint has wrecked the ability to present in the modern world. I seldom use it, and if so, only to have one slide every hour or so of presenting. Therefore, when you ask these "Bright Business People" on the show to present without their beloved PowerPoint, they do not know what to do. This is the only part of the show I do not laugh out loud at, because it is a serious flaw in our world today.

Let us make it how it should be – i.e. very simple and straightforward.

A pitch presentation should always follow the same three step process.

- Your Problem (which comes from market intelligence)
- Our Product (which is clear and connected to the problem)
- The Price (which should be totally clear)

There are only 6 reasons why people buy anything – I use my own acronym, which is SHAPER© to remember them –

Safety – it works, I have trust in the brand or product or I have heard good testimonials of you

Honour – the brand is great, I feel good owning it and it makes my life happier

Advancement – I love the new research and development that goes into it and I like being the first to own it

Protection – if (when) it goes wrong, you will look after me

Economy – value for money, return on investment

Relationship – I like you and I want to do repeat business with you

People will only recognise between one and three of these motivations.

People will always buy for the same reasons.

It does not change dependant on what you buy.

You can identify a 'SHAPER FOOTPRINT©' by clever questioning.

You don't have time to do this in a pitch.

People will believe that their buying motivations are the only ones, or the best ones and will sell to those.

In a pitch, you must mention them all, because your audience will be mixed.

When you structure a pitch, remember that Sir Winston Churchill said "Tell them what you are going to tell them, tell them and tell them what you have told them." This means you must have an introduction, a main body and an ending.

Introduction

Ever been to a presentation, meeting or training course and for some reason you cannot identify, not really liked it. This is because the introduction was done wrongly. Everyone, subconsciously and without knowing it, will ask themselves 5 questions at the beginning of any presentation, meeting or training course. They are –

- Who are you?

- What gives you the right to tell me this?
- How long do I have to sit here for?
- What's it about?
- What do you want me to do?

If these are not answered, quickly, you have lost everyone, but they will not know why. So, an introduction looks like this –

- I'm Matthew Quinn
- I have been a very successful sales person and sales manager for a number of years and now speak publicly about the subject on many occasions and levels for all types of industry
- I'll be speaking for about 45 minutes at which point we will have a break and discussion
- The topic today is negotiation and I will be covering
    o Planning
    o Power
    o The 5 forget me not rules of negotiation
    o Dirty tricks
- Please, ask questions at the end / during the presentation (does not matter which you use, so long as you tell people.)

"Everyone happy with that?"

The last sentence is what we call a link – everyone needs it to tell them when the introduction is over and when the main body starts. There are 2 reasons I use "Everyone happy with that?". First, because my personality, being quite relaxed, suits it – if you have one, use your own personality to come up with a link. Secondly, it is a psychological link – if I ask if you are happy with something and you say yes – I am allowed to carry on as I wish. Believe me, an experienced presenter will know if anyone in any audience, no matter how large, is not happy.

The main body is just as easy. You will notice my agenda above. I already know what my chapters are, so rather than devising one 45 minute presentation and writing the whole lot down, I devise 4 individual 10 minute presentations, anyone can talk for 10 minutes on a subject with which they are familiar, so why would they need notes? There you have one of the secrets of the presenting trade – we don't know a whole 45 minute presentation off by heart, but we do know 4, 6 or 8 smaller ones. Clever eh?

Make sure the main body is structured and you will not go far wrong. Remember – your problem, my solution – it makes so much sense.

"A speech is like a love affair, any fool can start one, but to end one takes considerable skill!" – Lord Mancroft, Conservative Peer.

The summary – arguably the most important part of a pitch and one that is not often messed up, because it is more often than not non existent. People finish their pitch and say – "any questions?" or "that's it" – this is very weak.

The summary must be six points long and must remind the audience of why they would buy it. Remember, there are only 6 reasons why people buy, so your last words are –

"So, in summary, you should buy the new dreamy dream mattress because – you can trust our brand's reputation, we have a fantastic place in people's perception, we use only the newest style fibres and springs, we have a world class customer service centre, we promise your investment will last for 15 years and we give great personal service in our stores!"

When you leave, each person will say – "I like them because……" the because will be different for each person, but that does not matter, as everyone is liking you and you will have hit each spot exactly!!!

Finally, nerves. Everyone gets them, they will never go away, if you say you are nervous before a presentation, you are normal. If you say you are not nervous, you are either mad, or a liar. Handle them by process and structure. Some tips for you –

- Don't make outrageous claims (This is a breakthrough in modern home fitness) in a presentation, they will get picked up on
- Don't read from notes, it amateurish
- Have some passion – I remember telling everyone I met as a customer in my car dealership that my parts manager held "*TWO* HUNDRED AND *FIFTY* THOUSANDS POUNDS WORTH OF STOCK!!!"" in his warehouse – I still to this day don't know whether that is a lot or not, but it sounded loads and we got many a deal from that simple fact back in those days…..
- It is not "the product" it has a name, use it
- Your gang should sit there with straight faces – you are all on the same side and do not, ever outnumber your customer. Everyone does not have to be there
- There are 5 elements of body language of which you should be aware – don't worry about anything else, they are –
    - Mirroring – be like your customer, if they wear a tracksuit and use jargon, be the same
    - Avoid barriers – never stand behind a lectern, or have a pad in front of your chest
    - Open stance – be comfortable, but move a little, if you feel better with your hands in your pockets,

- just put one in, it's a compromise between comfort and professionalism and it works
  - Smile – works wonders you know, and it's contagious
  - Eye contact – not just looking at everyone, but fixing the chief buyer (you should know who this is) with a sparkle of the eye when something good is being presented

Then comes negotiation – we will cover this in great detail later, I am sure. However, in the show, exclusivity came up, so let us focus on this for a moment.

Exclusivity is a concession – treat it as one. By that I mean, you should know it may come up, particularly in John Lewis, so be ready for it. Have a reasonable demand on hand to ask for. Bear in mind, if someone asks for exclusivity, they are interested in your product – dive on that.

Once again, Philip showed how poor he is at negotiation – please, never use him as your estate agent.

The buyer asked for exclusivity. Philip said –

"You'd have to make us a serious offer on some serious orders."

Now, just read that sentence again. I bet you could not tell me what he actually means. The reason you cannot tell me what it means? Because it means ABSOLUTELY NOTHING!!!! If someone said this to me in a negotiation, I would crush them. The buyer responded quite kindly, I think, by asking what a serious offer was. Philip them started to stumble.....

Rule one of Negotiation –

HE WHO BIDS FIRST WINS!

Always!

I would have said the following.

"Exclusivity? Brilliant – that sounds like a deal. How about an order for 12,000 units for 12 months exclusivity?" (Of course I would already know how many they would be thinking of selling a month, because my marketing people would have told me.)

Thank God for Jasmina, she took the mantle and went in, a little too high and a little too short on the time, admittedly, however at least she showed some business sense. Her team let her down straight away though. When the buyer said that it was too short a time – I would have asked "well how long do you need to order 20,000?"

Think of the psychology behind it. Jasmina asked for an order of 20,000 units for a period of six months. The man said it was too short. HE DID NOT SAY IT WAS TOO MANY UNITS – ASSUME THAT HE WANTS 20,000 AND WORK ON THE OTHER AREA.

Then the other buyer said that it was not "a particularly good deal." So why not ask what is – this is a business discussion after all.

All it takes is some thought.

In summary, in this type of task, in The Apprentice and in real life, split your team into three

- Design, to work out industry knowledge
- Market, to get customer knowledge
- Sell to get business knowledge

I'd have won this one. By a long way.

Boardroom Tactics

I have an awful feeling that Philip is going to do well in this series. Not because he is any good in business, he is terrible. However, he is playing the game like a star. Sir Alan actually congratulates him and the pathetic Lorraine on winning the task. It was clearly the work of Jasmina that got them the 10,000 orders from John Lewis. She went in with 20,000 and came out with 10,000 – not bad. I'll say well done to her, but I'll also be placing a bet on Philip getting to the interview stage, sadly.....

I'll skip straight to the final three, as I am sure you know remember the tactics for the first boardroom stages.

Ben has been brought back to the boardroom. He is becoming annoying, as always happens with someone around this time – on any reality show. He'll be out soon, no matter how well he does as he will be in the boardroom more times than anyone else. Remember Birmingham Jo last year – not a bad girl, but infuriatingly annoying.

So we have the three in the firing line – no surprises that it is Ben, Maj and James.

Ben is becoming awful, but for now, showing good TV skills. His catch phrase of "Let me finish" will soon turn up on a t shirt somewhere. This will not save him much longer though, Sir Alan will soon be bored with him, probably by the 4th time he is in the boardroom, which, by my guess will be 3 weeks time. I'll put a bet on that he is there next week. He is a good hate figure for the moment, but it will wear.

Maj has nothing to say and looks sad all the time.

James is an amiable fool, which in a weird way is good TV, but again, not for long.

Week Three – the result!

Business – wise, James would have gone, followed by Ben, who only reaches second chop because he did, after all, come up with the only idea – Maj would survive as the best of a bad lot.

However, as we now know, this is not business but TV……

Maj – you're fired! Once again, Sir Alan, good choice, for a TV show, I approve!

Chapter 5

"Leadership potential?"

This is a key point in the show, by this point, Sir Alan has made his line in the sand about the basics. He knows now who he wants to watch and who he wants to lose. He will know the final 4 by now and will not tolerate anyone making a mistake on basics. Anyone with any skill at all will accelerate from here – the total losers have gone and the hidden people are about to go, anyone who has come into the show ready to learn, i.e. TO BE AN APPRENTICE will now do well.

It is exactly the same in business, don't try to run before you can walk. Have a look back at the previous four chapters in this book – they are there for a reason, they are the basics. Once you have a good foundation of business skills, you can start to implement them well. I left the Army with some of the best leadership training in the world, having spent time at the Royal Military Academy Sandhurst – however, I told few people this when I went into civilian life – why? Because nobody is interested. They want to see what you can do, not what you have done. I spent a few years learning and working hard to understand business, costs, sales, marketing, presenting and then, only then I moved on to leading others to do it.

All projects include the basics, if you have a basis of these skills then you can manage any project – however, one of the things you need to be aware of is exactly what Sir Alan is looking for from here on, which is the basics of management and leadership.

This is exactly why Sir Alan chose, and always will choose at this point the team "leaders". He was making a point, i.e. choosing the weakest (of a pretty bad bunch...). Watch the episode again and listen to what Sir Alan says about the basics of the task –

"The profit margin in cosmetics is massive, it should be made for pennies and sold for pounds."

He is dead right, however, as he knows, this is not what this task is about. It is about spotting someone he can mould into a future leader.

Here is what I would like you to do now. Think of a great leader – the first one that pops into your mind. Now get a pen and paper and write down all the specific characteristics of that leader, in your opinion. What makes them the person they are? Do this, properly and thoughtfully, before you read on.

Now, look at Noorul and Paula and how they lead their teams. Write down, or tick off the leadership characteristics you wrote down that they show. I bet the second list is short...

The reason I ask you to do this is that everyone knows the correct answer. Standard list items that come up are –

- Charisma
- Courage (of convictions)
- Confidence
- Vision
- Integrity
- Enthusiasm

- Belief
- Imagination

All great leaders have these things, whether you agree with their intent or not – I dislike Tony Blair's policies, however I accept that he is a good leader, mainly due to his charisma, with the press and public. Margaret Thatcher had nothing if not belief and courage, as did Winston Churchill. Alex Ferguson has vision and enthusiasm – you get my point. All of these can be developed by someone like Sir Alan Sugar, but the spark needs to be there first and with Noorul and Paula, it's not even a smoulder…

Sir Alan is no longer looking for the basics, the candidates should have these already so you will be discounted immediately without them. Again, this is the same in business, work on the basics, then develop your leadership.

Let's have a look at the specifics of what happened on the show – the two project managers (there is a reason why I have suddenly changed their title from 'leader') sat down with their teams in the first instance to generate ideas. Bear in mind they were discussing cosmetics and the basics and actions outlined in the previous chapters still apply, splitting the team, setting objectives, sales skills and the like. However, as a project manager, your role is to enable the team to start the process. Noorul did a lamentable job – particularly for someone who claims to be a 'natural leader'. This meeting should be driven, his was stilted, dry and embarrassing, which got them off to a bad start. He lost control, was uninspiring and demotivated his team. Paula's meeting was more well managed, but her mistake (in this case, fatal for her) was to abdicate responsibility at the start.

As a boss, you are not expected to be an expert on everything, merely to understand the processes and importance of everything. For Paula to announce that she is no expert in costings is acceptable. For her to give the role to someone else and then forget about it is not.

Delegation is the ability to give someone the authority to do your job, whilst you maintain the responsibility, if Paula had understood this, she would have been fine. Jasmina and Ben were very clearly told to keep Paula "on track". This, again, means nothing – great business people are never vague, they are always specific. If she had told the two of them what parameters they should work with, what to identify and how to report back, it would have been different. By different I mean that the mistake either would not have happened, or if it did, the fault would have a specific place to lie.

Here is the key with this task. Sir Alan is not, in fact, yet, looking for a leader. He is looking for a manager. There is a huge difference between the roles. One cannot survive without the other, however, you need to be sure which role you are doing. Many businesses fail these days because we want everyone to be a leader – as soon as some spark is seen, we appoint the person as 'the leader'.

The Army is great at this differentiation. Ask any soldier who does more work, the Sergeant or the Officer and the reply will always be the same – the Sergeant, however, there is huge respect for the Officer's authority. In a soldier's eyes, this man controls the raging force that is the Sergeant and they cannot believe that one person would have so much power. The Sergeant assigns guard duties, creates rotas, checks supplies, assigns tasks and watches resources, the Officer guides everyone to the vision. This should be the same in business. Look at the characteristic list below –

Leader	Manager
Has vision vision	Works to the business

Supports managers	Oversees work done
Motivates	Manages
Allows creativity	Follows processes
Observes	Monitors
Navigates	Drives
Keeps command	Keeps discipline

For this task, process is needed, so therefore a manager is needed. Sir Alan knows this, as do all great business leaders. If you are in a position of authority over another person or group of people, make a decision as to whether you need to be a leader or a manager and work to that.

The winner, in business as opposed to this task, is the leader who knows they have excellent levels of management below them to do the job. Just consider Sir Fred Goodwin for a moment... A good leader with poor managers, a poor leader with good managers or a poor leader with poor managers – you decide for yourself. However, once you have decided, ask yourself what would you have done in his place with a business like RBS and how would you have made it different?

Interestingly, I mentioned the Army a moment ago and you will see that the odious Ben is back on form – now he is telling us that he gained a scholarship to Sandhurst... I am always amazed how many failed Army Officers turn up on this show – there were three last year – and do terribly. If you are one of these people, remember, getting to Sandhurst shows you have a glimmer of potential – you are only close to the finished product when you pop out of the other end. If you did not go to the Academy, don't mention it, it devalues what others have done, as well as that, nobody in civilian life cares anyway.

Back to the task in hand…

With a good manager, the cedarwood and sandalwood mix up would not have happened – this is what lost the task for Paula's group, who had, let's face it, the best product, by far.

Noorul was finding making any decision difficult, which caused some friction, most notably the arguments between Philip and Kimberley. Let me make 2 points here –

1 – Never, ever, ever, argue like that in front of other people, it is astoundingly bad form.

2 – Philip, he is a useless pleb, however, I have an awful feeling that his excellent game playing will get him far in this show. However, he accuses Kimberley of having no opinion. Sadly for him, the person with whom he is dealing is an American, their culture is not one of forceful opinions, they are fearful of political correctness. It is vital in business to understand another person's culture and deal with it – i.e. make the decisions yourself.

For once, I saw a glimmer of good management in one of our candidates – Debra spotted the mistake on the fragrances – sadly, Paula shot her down without knowing the facts. From then, she was doomed!

Noorul on the other hand continues to lose control, he has the tiresome Philip shouting down the phone at him about amounts of honey – this is where discipline comes in, Noorul should have closed him down immediately.

There are one or two real lessons here –

- Keep control
- Avoid euphemisms, if you are a leader, be one, but do not confuse the title of leader and manager

- Successful people are never vague, always specific, ensure that your people know exactly what is expected of them and remind them constantly
- Make decisions, do not dither over things that are of little importance
- Prioritise
- Be very clear on what your resources are
- Take responsibility

This last point is shown famously by the moment where Nick Hewer points out the fragrance mistake – Paula immediately pointed the finger at Debra and Ben, this set the hares running, everyone immediately started to plan how they could distance themselves from the mistake. Blaming is a useless action which comes from the culture of today, it is a constant shame on our society that we watch commercials on the television asking –

"Had an accident, not your fault?"

The definition of an accident is that it is not your fault, however, would it not be good to have children learning how to take responsibility? Have some guts, determination and integrity and your business life will grow exponentially.

Take my advice, it is good to get knocked down once or twice in this life, it shows you how to get up again.

A good manager would have fixed the problem first and then been very clear on what went wrong and why. If that manager had assigned tasks properly at the start, all would have been well.

It is interesting that Ben blames everyone else immediately, even though the costings were assigned (vaguely) to him at the beginning – I can see why he did not complete Sandhurst, I would not want him next to me if the shooting started…

This particular mistake was a real shame, as Paula's product was far superior to Noorul's – in fact for the whole remainder of the task Paula's team was far better, but they had shot themselves with the cost – basic, basics, basics.

An example is the look of the teams whilst selling – Paula's team look smart, professional, trustworthy, Noorul's are dressed up again. Paula's team have a good pitch spot, Noorul's team are all over the place. Paula is selling, Noorul is a sap with no decision making skills. Paula is listening to her team (apart from in the example below) but Noorul is trying to over control – Howard is giving him the facts and he wants to see the ground before making a decision – trust your advisers! If it was not for the cost mistake, it would have been Noorul, Kim and Philip in the boardroom and it would have been the end of Noorul.

An interesting business mistake from Paula was not being brave enough. James, in a rare moment of brilliance, suggests he could sell the product for a fiver – Paula knocked him back to £4.50 – if he thinks he can do it, let him try. Personally, I would rather spend a fiver than walk off with another 50 pence piece rattling about I my pocket.

Finally, sitting in a cab in order to join your team on an empty street is a bad move. However, finding a dealer to take the rest of your stock is a good one – well done James.

In summary, this task, like so much in business is about the difference between leadership and management and is so easy to get wrong remember –

- Learn the basics, then manage, then lead
- Control the process
- Be specific, never vague
- Trust your advisers, but give them parameters

- Keep discipline
- Set an example

Boardroom Tactics

Little to say on this chapter – all three were fighters, Ben is being an overbearing bully, which Sir Alan does not like, however, it is, again, cringingly good television – he's got another couple of weeks from that. Sadly though, the decision was always going to be the same…

Week Four – the result!

This was a real shame as it was always clear that Paula was going to go as she held responsibility for the loss, even though the product was far better and Paula herself was one of the more pleasant candidates. I don't think she had a chance to shine, she is clearly a better business person than the fool Ben, however, she does not make such good television. Ben will survive a couple of more weeks because of his awful personality and I have to admit, that Jasmina is quite good in places.

Therefore – Paula, your fired! Again, regrettably, the right result.

Chapter Six

"Commercial Sense – good or pants?"

Commercials, advertisements, straplines. They are everywhere. It seems to me that this particular task, again one that comes up time and time again on The Apprentice, should be the most straightforward. I say this for two reasons. Firstly, as I say, this task will always appear on the show. The reason for this is simple, Sir Alan has built a business empire by designing and selling new branded items. Whether they are any good or not is debatable, however he needs to know to whom to sell these items and what makes them buy. I could almost guarantee that you have never seen an Amstrad telephone advertised on the television – this is because the customer that is needed for this product does not buy through television advertising and Sir Alan knows this – or at least one of his people does. This brings me to the second reason why this task should be one of the simpler ones, we are all customers. If the so called business brains on the show were to think like a customer for a moment, they would see how these things should be done.

I think this may be a short chapter. Let's begin like this –

Get a pen and paper and write down 4 advertisements, or straplines, or jingles that you remember – think fast and quick and do not try to choose your favourite.

Now depending on your age, I could bet that the list below contains one or more of your list –

- It does what it says on the tin!
- Just do it!
- They're tasty tasty very very tasty!
- The milky bars are on me!
- Happiness is…..!
- The Coco pops chimp (Coco)

This tells me that commercials or straplines fall into 2 categories, if they are successful.

– I remember the product
– I remember the advert

Now, clearly, the intent is for you to remember the product. So ask yourself, what were "Tasty, tasty, very very tasty."? (For a bonus point, tell me the actor that sang the song – answers on a postcard.)

If you remember the advert, but not the product, has it worked? Well, some would say yes, because if nothing else, you are building a product awareness, if not the awareness of a specific brand. This means that when you go to the supermarket wanting something that was "tasty…etc" you will go to the cereal stand and then see the product that you saw on the TV.

However, for me, in business, that is not good enough. I want people to come and ask for my product specifically. I'm guessing that Sir Alan is looking for the same attitude.

This particular episode of the show is great because the business analogies with this task are clear. The brief was simple – develop a brand for a new cereal and sell it to health conscious parents and their kids. So many times, people have failed in their tasks for not reading the brief properly – this was a prime example. Kimberley, a self styled marketing guru rushed straight down the wrong path – she immediately went into "design a character" mode. Is it only me that sees where she has gone wrong?

Kate's team actually sat down and started with their product – they already knew their market, Sir Alan had told them. The next step is product and the campaign and character appear when the need requires, not before. Coco the monkey appeared in support of Coco Pops cereal, it was only much later when he was a strong enough brand himself that he began to sell other cereals through his persona.

You cannot build a character and then design a brand around it, the market audience for that is too narrow – Kimberley's biggest mistake here was to allow the terrible Philip to smash his ideas into the room, coming up with a lamentable character and leaving no time for the brand itself. Again, he shows his immaturity and naivety in business.

Kate split her team and went to look at some competitor cereals – a simple, yet indispensible part of the process. Actually looking at some successful brands with a competitor's point of view, rather than a consumer point of view is probably one of the things that won Kate the task.

Kimberley's team at this point were trying to wrestle a poor character into a rudimentary brand in order to catch up on the time they wasted arguing. This resulted in a poor character, worse box (green – for cereal????) and a terrible commercial.

<u>Building a Brand</u>

<u>Best Way (Kate's Team)</u>

Market (End user (for proof and information) AND distributor)

Product (What does it do? How does it look?)

Style (What fits with the above that will impress our market?)

Brand (So how can we make it blend together, colours, finish, information)

Sell (Let's go and see our buyers (NOT THE END USERS!!))

<u>The Bad Way (Kimberley's Team)</u>

Market (They looked at the end user without thinking of the distributors)

Style (Thought of a character and then dumped the job onto the designer)

Brand (There wasn't one)

Product (Vague)

Sell (Cannot do)

This task was TO BUILD A BRAND. Not a character. In business it is exactly the same. If you have a new brand, follow the process in the same way as Kate's team and you will move forward well.

With marketing, as with sales, there is very much a process to follow, otherwise your customer will not know why they are buying the product. This means that they will not buy your product.

Once you have a brand and then a character identified, you can embark on your marketing, or in this case, design your commercial.

Remember, there are only 6 reasons why people buy –

Safety – I trust the brand and I can see proof of longevity

Honour – I like the image and would like to associate with it

Advancement – it's new and I like research and development

Protection – I want to be looked after as a consumer

Economy – return on investment or value for money

Relationship – I like the person selling to me

In business you don't know to whom you are selling, so your marketing has to do one of two things. Either choose the aspects of a SHAPER © footprint towards which your product has a natural bent, or try and cover them all. In the task, it has been said quite clearly that Sir Alan is the client – so your advertising has to be geared towards HIM and him alone.

Sir Alan has told you he wants a product that he knows will work (healthy parents) so go for Safety ("This is what this product does and here is the proof!"). He also likes brand awareness and wants to feel that there is life in that (building your character after the product will do this – the parrot pirate was good idea) – therefore these are the areas on which to focus for your advertisement and your pitch.

Which of course, takes me on to the pitch.

Why can nobody, ever, appearing on The Apprentice do a presentation. Just a thought – if you believe you are a business brain, presenting is one of the minimal skills you should have. If you see it as a skill you lack, get in touch with me and I will help you. It is the only thing that still annoys me about The Apprentice, because it is so basic.

This type of pitch should take very little time to prepare well. For Kimberley to say that there is not time for her to prepare the pitch is outrageous. If you have designed, developed and brought to life a brand new product, you should be able to stand up and tell people about that with little or no preparation. I buy on Honour, Protection and Relationship so a pitch missing in depth knowledge of why a brand new product was good for me would turn me off straight away.

When giving this pitch to your distributors (remember, at this point, Sir Alan is not judging you, he is leaving that to the advice of his colleagues, who are your buyers) the main thing you need is PASSION – these people want to know why OTHER people will buy your product, that is the level on which they think. So tell them.

Take Debra for example – far too uptight for this kind of pitch. Sadly for her, she has one of those faces that rests at a scowl, this is why she often looks quite unattractive. For her to lead this pitch is a bizarre choice. I'll give you a clear example – there is a study of what is known as 'incongruent communication' it states that if you say something, whilst your body language is saying something else then you are 'incongruent' or 'mixed'. The result is that nobody will agree to what you are saying, but they won't know why.

Debra said the word "FUN", twice, neither time with even the hint of a smile on her face. This, dear reader is 'incongruent', as well as being very poor. The icing on the cake was that she read the whole pitch from a book – why should I believe anyone who is pitching their own product to me and not only needs NOTES, but also has the ineptitude to read them from a huge book held in front of her chest!

Debra was challenged by the advertising lady in the crowd as to who her customers were – she was quite right, and at that moment in time your customers were the ones in the audience, the buyers from supermarkets. Supermarkets will think of a number of things with a new product –

- Can I sell it quickly?
- How much shelf space need I give it?
- Does it stand out (in a good way)?
- Will my customer put it in their basket?

In the same was each customer type will have their own questions. In your business you need to identify the questions and answer them.

The most frustrating thing about this particular pitch was the missed opportunity on the communication of the idea.

Whenever you give a presentation, you should remember that people communicate in only 5 ways – these communication types follow the 5 senses.

Visual – what we see

Auditory – what we hear

Kinaesthetic – what we feel

Olfactory – what we smell

Gustatory – what we taste

Remember VAKOG whenever you put together a presentation. Most people will be heavily versed toward one area, usually in the first three. I am heavily auditory, this means I like presentations where people just tell me things, I hate slideshows and demonstrations and I learn nothing from video clips or making my own notes. I cannot do a mind map and if I write anything down during a training course or presentation, I have no idea what it means later.

Some people are heavily visual and like slides, flipcharts, colours etc and some people are heavily kinaesthetic, so they enjoy break out groups, props and demonstrations. It is VITAL that you know what you are. This is because you will naturally fall into this style when presenting – I will naturally just stand there and talk, I must remember never to do this because I will alienate everyone in my audience who is not auditory. IT IS THE AUDIENCE THAT MATTERS! So, whether you disagree with handing a box around during your presentation or not – do it for the kinaesthetic people. It is the only way you will put your message across.

Example. Someone said to me once – I would never hand out examples of my product during a presentation, because some people just sit there and play with it, rather than listening to you. I always give things out at the end.

This is hogwash – the people who are playing with the example are kinaesthetic, meaning they are learning whilst fiddling with your product. As kinaesthetic people, they are not listening to you anyway, so give them what they want and your message will rush into them as if you had beamed it straight into their mind. Similar examples can be given for all the types – people love flipcharts, people love to hear music to learn, people need information on slides – all correct, but only for the individual types.

We know this is true, how many times have you seen a picture that reminds you of a holiday, or heard a song that makes you think of a great night out, or felt a blanket that reminds you of a person, or smelled food that makes you think of a holiday or tasted sweets that remind you of walking home from school???? It works, see.

The missed opportunity here? These people were talking about food – look at what Kate's team did when they began the task, they got the cereal out and felt it, tasted it and smelled it, they then built the brand around it. Need I prove this again? this could have been a wonderful pitch – look –

V – Here is what our box looks like and why we have chosen the colours

A – Here is our song, or jingle

K – Here is our box for you to play with, or some of the cereal for you to feel

O – Smell it – it's food!

G – Taste it – it's food!

Imagine how much more powerful that would have been, instead of Debra and Mona looking glum and just saying random words at the audience.

Finally on the pitch. Questions at the end of a pitch can make or break it. If they are done well a bad pitch can become great and if they are done badly a great pitch can be ruined. Let's look at 2 examples during the session of questions.

Kate – thanked the person for the question, answered it properly, was clear, polite and confident and then – brilliantly, asked if that answered the question. Perfect!

Philip – just argued with his potential customer and was then put in his place. Utter stupidity.

I hope you have learned something from those two examples.

It was pretty clear all the way through who would win.

Boardroom Tactics

Here we see Philip playing the game again, taking the leader's side ("Kimberley was a good team leader") in the hope he will not be brought into the firing line – he is very good at this part of the show and if he concentrated these efforts on the actual tasks, he might be quite good. However I think he knows exactly what he is doing, that is making up for poor business acumen and task performance by playing a good game in the boardroom. Sir Alan will see through him soon enough. It is, however, a shame that Ben got away with being on the winning team as I would have liked to see how he fared against Kate in the boardroom.

Lorraine however is playing an odd game. Honesty, particularly at this point of the show, whilst a great and certainly required trait in business is an absolutely foolish card to play in the boardroom. At best, it will mean you end up in the firing line, at worst, that you are fired due to being a trouble maker.

Kate at this point has been rightly praised – she did well and I hope she goes further, Sir Alan is now starting to spot the game players.

In the firing line, we had Kimberley just saying words which mean little and being melodramatic, which is the culture of her country. She was claiming that she manages creativity and needs substance to work on in a business – just go back and watch that and write down what you think she means – can't do it? No, neither can I. There was, at that point, no doubt in my mind who would go.

Lorraine is sticking to her guns and Sir Alan likes this, whereas Philip is just being offensive.

Strangely, it was clear who Kimberley was going to bring in, although the real deserving firing line people were set free –

Mona – a terrible pitch and very little else

Noorul – was he in this episode?

Howard – pointless

Any of these in the firing line and Kimberley would have stayed. On a purely business point of view, Philip needs to go, I would not employ him to wash my driveway. Although, he is good TV, as is Lorraine, for different reasons.

Week Five – the result!

Sadly, due to poor boardroom choices and not very good TV for a British audience, Kimberley – you're fired.... Correct choice again.

Chapter Seven

"The devil's in the detail"

Never underestimate the importance of two areas in business. One is ensuring that you are clear on all the details and the other is the value of your product or service to other people. Both of these things were ignored in this episode of the show.

I remember being a car salesman, back in the mid nineties, for a Peugeot dealer just after I left the army. I'd been away on holiday for a couple of weeks with some friends and I turned up at the dealership on my first day back, a little early to deal with the inevitable paperwork, to find my boss waiting for me on the used car pitch. He was visibly excited.

"I'm so glad you're back." He said. "I've got something for you!"

He led me to the workshop and pressed the button to raise the door. As the door slowly slid into the roof, he continued:

"We got this in part exchange the day you went away. I've been hiding this in here ever since, because it's yours to sell – you'll get the most money for it, I'm sure."

The door opened to reveal one of the nicest, and rarest cars of the time. A Peugeot 309 Goodwood. It had black leather seats, a dark green paint finish and wooden steering wheel and gearstick. It was lovely. One thing Peugeot are very good at is making their special editions look special, as well as keeping the numbers down to drive desire. I think there were less than 200 of these cars in the country, most of which had been stolen, or crashed, and we had one!

Best of all, it was fast. Really, really fast.

Dave, the boss, knew that I would get passionate about this car and would only sell it to the right person at the right price. This is why he kept it for me.

I gave the paperwork mound to someone else to do and immediately got on the telephone. One call to a previous prospect got me an interested party coming in. Two hours for me to 'familiarise' myself with the car and then one hour to sell it to the man. The profit margin was great, we had finance and a warranty on the car and we also had a very happy customer. In fact, he sold the car about three years later as he was joining the Navy and told me how sorry he was to see it go. However, his bank manager was quite happy, he sold it for only about £500 less than he bought it from me for…

It was from Dave the sales manager, because of things like this, that I learned what the word 'value' actually meant. I also learned the difference between 'cost money' and 'lost money'. It is in this chapter that we will investigate these areas.

'Lost money' comes from being careless, however it is often unavoidable because things outside your control happen. 'Cost money' is avoidable and therefore unforgiveable. This is because you 'cost money' for yourself when you do something which results in you getting less than you could have, or should have in a business deal. Not because of anything untoward, but because you have not sold something at the right PRICE because of the right VALUE. The reasons are normally poor negotiation, bad pricing, the wrong buyer or the wrong seller, but most of all it is because as a seller you don't see the value of the sale item.

Dave knew this – that is why he waited for 2 weeks to sell the Goodwood. If my colleague, Stuart, had been allowed to sell it, he would have parked it by the road for people to see and then, in his true style, discounted it for the first person who showed any interest in it. This is not selling, it is taking orders.

Sir Alan also understands this. This is why this task is in the show – so he can see who he can trust to manage the value of what they are selling. It sounds simple, and it is, but it is also easy to mess it up.

You cannot run a business without understanding about 'cost money' and how to avoid it.

Also in this task, Sir Alan is demonstrating how easy it is to run off down the wrong path. He is also seeing through Ben and Philip which is why he has chosen them as project managers. He knows that they will rush headlong into the task without properly reading the brief, which means he will have a good chance of getting rid of one of them.

Time an time again on the show, the candidates are told to read the brief. Time an time again it is ignored. If you decide to go on this show, every time there is a dossier given to you, which is every task, read it thoroughly, looking for the twist in the task – it will save an awful lot of grief.

Just in case you the viewer did not realise, the brief said that each item had a value – sell as many items as possible for MORE THAN THE VALUE. The value of the items will be removed from the income and the team with the highest remainder (or, in this case, lowest loss) will win. What could be simpler?

This will scare you... if either team had sold NOTHING in this task – they would have won, with a net of zero... Ponder that for a moment and decide whether these are the brightest business talents of Great Britain.

What the brief did not say was run off and sell everything for whatever you can get. Simple value understanding is the key.

Both teams 'cost money' for Sir Alan because they sold their items for less than their value – never mind making a profit.

Here are the simple business lessons of this task –

Sir Alan said; "Your job is to FIND OUT what each item is worth, then go and sell it."

He actually told the candidates what to do and in what order...

Therefore the process is –

- Define the value of your product
    - How much did it cost you?
    - How do you transport or package it?
    - Who will buy it?
    - Is there an expert valuer I can ask?
    - What would people pay for it?
    - How long will it take me to sell?

All these areas define value – interestingly, Ben seemed to spot this as team leader, but then he did not instruct his people in how to do it. Therefore, the value aspect did not matter to people because they had not had to work to figure it out. This comes down to personal value – how much do I care about it? In Ben's team, the answer was 'not a jot!'. Therefore, value is lost in desperation to sell, which is where people commonly go wrong. Strange behaviour for a man who can keep his head when bullets, explosions and casualties are happening around him...

Next step in the process –

- Sell your product with a mark up
    - Choose your buyer
        - Where are they?
        - Have they got funds?
        - Will they attempt to bargain?
    - Understand why the buyer would love your product by enquiring after their needs.
    - Define your absolute lowest price – BEFORE you bargain

Value or Cost Price + (effort of sale + transfer) + reasonable profit
= Minimum Sale Price

- Define your optimum pricing

Minimum Sale Price + Extra Profit

No matter what the persuasion, NEVER, EVER, NEVER, EVER go below your pre determined minimum. If you were confident enough in the calculation prior to the sales discussion, stick with it. By the way, for those who follow Lorraine on this show – reasonable profit is not hundreds of thousands of pounds... remember the definition of selling.

Noorul and his skeleton give a great example of this. The customer said "I'm a student", twice. Suddenly, £159.99 +VAT became £60. you could actually see the desperation to sell in their faces. On another note, why was it, to a private customer £159.99 +VAT? – nobody would believe this price. Why not simply £185 – it sounds more realistic.

In The Apprentice, costing Sir Alan money will normally cost you the task. In business it is only something to do when you are going out of business, otherwise it will cause you to go out of business!

Of course, some people may argue that it is easy to identify a value if you have a product to sell such as a car, a book or a sofa, but it is more difficult if you are selling a service – not so!

When I led a team of consultants we sold time, in parcels of a day. Clearly I had to make a profit, but how to work out the value of my day?

Take for example a junior consultant, who I would pay a salary of £75,000 a year, including bonus. The cost to me of this individual is around £125,000 a year. Most of their expenses are taken up by the customer, so I can ignore these. Therefore the junior consultant costs me £342 every day of the year. However, they will only be utilised (that is customer facing or chargeable time) for 110 days of the year, which means that every utilised day costs me £1,136. In theory, the customer will have cost me around £10,000 to sell to in the first place, with marketing, visits and proposals. I need to recoup this within the first year of the relationship In that year I would hope to sell 20 days to that customer. That means, to recoup my cost, I should add £500 to each day.

This means that the total value for each day sold in the first year is £1,636.00. If I sell for any less than this, I'm costing myself money. On top of this, I need to make a reasonable profit. If I want a minimum of 15% profit, I must sell each day for £1,880.00. I'd like, of course, to make more, so I start my proposals at £2,150.00 plus VAT per day and I know I have a sustainable business, so long as the minimum I ever sell a day at is £1,880.00 plus VAT.

Therefore – whatever you are selling, follow these rules –

- DEFINE THE VALUE
- IDENTIFY YOUR LOWEST PRICE
- SET YOUR SALE PRICE
- FIND YOUR CUSTOMER
- NEVER, EVER UNDERSELL

Boardroom Tactics

Let's be clear on this episode. Sir Alan chose Ben and Philip because he wanted rid of them – they are clearly running their course of good TV and need to go before they embarrass themselves in the interview stage. Philip is ignorant and simple whereas Ben is delusional. If it had not been for one, horrid comment from Noorul, Ben would have been off our screens and into the Daily Star for good.

Ben shows off his real indecisiveness when choosing who to bring back (decisions under fire Ben???), more important he showed his weakness by his blustering and changing his mind around James. Under pressure he crumbles, but made a great choice in Noorul. Clearly, Debra is too vicious to win, but Noorul is out of his depth completely and it is getting embarrassing, like an ill pet, he needs putting down. Poor TV and poor business is not what is needed on the show.

Noorul, however, holds one point of interest. Nick Hewer seems fascinated by him. I was convinced he hated him, but now feel that he actually likes him as a person and feels very sorry for him and is trying to help him move on.

Debra is viscous, petulant and abusive, she is trying to be cool, like one of the horrid girls at school who is not quite good looking enough to be of interest to the boys and not quite funny enough to be the friendly one. It makes good TV now, and will make even better TV when the interviewers make mincemeat of her, the panel will detest her.

Any of these three would have been a great one to fire, they are an awful trio. Ben though, was on his way out, having become very transparent in his inadequacies. One comment from Noorul saved him.

This shows us that there is a time in The Apprentice, as in business, to shut up. Sir Alan was turning Ben inside out and was about to fire him, until Noorul played the card that Ben wants fame. Now, this is probably true, he has no chance anywhere else, but what Noorul forgets is that if this is true, Sir Alan will know this and is powerful enough, if he wants, to make sure it never happens. For Noorul to use this as a tactic shows pure desperation, spite and immaturity. You'll notice that Debra knows this and clams up, for once completely, happy in the knowledge who is going to go, just for annoying Sir Alan.

Week Six – the result!
I think Noorul is a nice man and probably a good teacher, but it was time to go..... Noorul, you're fired – good choice again Sir Alan.

Chapter Eight

"Your order book is empty..."

I love it when a point is proven. I have been suspecting, particularly since Noorul's attack on Ben last week, that a large number of these candidates are people who really want to be on Big Brother but deem themselves above it. This was proved during this great episode where everyone is sure that they are going abroad and packs accordingly and then is so downtrodden when they see their fate!

Why is this important? Simple. It proves that these people have been watching the previous series of The Apprentice and only taken from it what they wanted to – to wit – "I may get famous", (Ruth Badger was hankering after my business this week, asking for £5,000 for a 45 minute speech. I asked her if she was selling herself as a business guru or a celebrity speaker, she struggled to answer...needless to say, we didn't commission her) or alternatively – "I get the chance of going abroad for a day or two on the tasks".

My recommendation at the start of this book was to get the previous series on DVD and watch it end to end. This recommendation still stands, however, please, watch them for the business and game playing lessons, not for the outcome of a few candidates!

Sir Alan announced this task as being about everyone selling. However, as always there was a twist, which most of the candidates missed, particularly the team leaders. That twist was that the task was really all about understanding the supply chain and your distributors business.

Many industries and businesses have distributors, whether it be fast moving consumer goods, hardware, financial services or vehicles, the process is the same. Sadly for the candidates, this simple task showed who was adept, or otherwise at this basic business need.

Sir Alan set up two appointments. A large hardware store and a designer home store (Heal's). These are the key, they are warm, ready and large appointments. Your audience for the pitch will be decision makers and they will be there to listen. If you insult them, you will get nothing. Sadly, our candidates were very poor.

If some time had been spent on researching the appointments, the candidates would have seen what the distributor's business is like. Let me demonstrate –

I know that Heal's in Manchester is

- A store which opened first in 1810 so has a long history – they know what they're doing
- A store which believes that they are the home of modern, designer and contemporary furniture
- Proud of the fact that they have won the 'cool brands' awards
- A store which boasts "Better furniture for better times"

How do I know this? I typed "Heal's Manchester" into Google and looked at their website for 30 seconds.

Armed just with this information, I know that Heal's WILL NOT buy a cat play house made from cardboard, nor will they buy a sleeping bag with arms and legs (although I would), nor a dog lead for lovers, nor a bike bag. They would buy hundreds of tap design coat racks and dozens of zipped ball chairs. How powerful would this task have been if the candidates had spent a little more time on research and less on feeling important with people pitching at them. It is too easy in business to get carried away feeling important. Next time you are on a flight, watch who turns their phone on the moment the flight lands and waits impatiently for the first bleep of a message. Let me tell you, nobody is that important, if you were, you'd have your own aircraft. However, the people who act like this think they are important and probably spend a lot of time missing the detail.

The second day of opportunity to sell door to door was a typical apprentice red herring. The first day was where all the opportunity is, for huge orders, because the right people are there – just like in your business.

Let's have a look at how this can work in practice.

If you have some appointments set up, you can decide on what you will pitch to them by understanding their needs. For this we use a system called the hierarchy of business needs.

Firstly, and very important, is the fact that you have to segment your distributor properly. Jasmina continually called the distributor "The Client". They are not a client, they are a customer – the difference is key. We have different words so we can treat them differently, not better or worse, just differently. A client receives professional services from one point of contact. A customer is more of a business partner with a number of people in the process. Actions, words attitudes and processes are different for each type. If one of my people got the two confused like Jasmina did, I would be very suspicious about their ability.

A hierarchy of business needs works on the assumption that every business, in every industry has the same primary need –

To make profit

We all know this and we are all working towards it. If this were not true, then it would not be a business. Therefore, poor distribution partners will talk about this incessantly. How much you will make because of this idea etc. The good business person will know that this shows a lack of imagination and research and will dismiss your ideas straight away. Ask yourself – how many times have you put the telephone down on someone who asks if you want to save money on your gas? In the cold light of day, this is madness, everyone wants to save money, in the same way that all businesses want to make a profit – so why put the phone down? The same reasons that the business owner does not want, yet, to hear you talking about the profit he'll make.

The secondary business needs are always similar, business to business and industry to industry, with some subtle changes. However, they all lead up to profit. Secondary needs are normally things like –

Margin, Turnover, Invoicing etc

Similarly, with these secondary needs, they will not help you fully understand the business.

In order to get really under the skin of a business, have some really key business conversations, pitch an idea well and ultimately be in a strong negotiating position for orders, you must have a really clear idea on the supporting needs. The issue here being that supporting needs are specific to industry sectors, and in some cases even specific businesses. If we looked at a supermarket, for example, the supporting needs could be –

Shelf Space, Brand Protection, Local Visibility, Average Shopping Basket, Constant Supply, Seasonal Ranges, Wide Product Choice, Bargain Bin Items, Checkout Efficiency, Trading Laws… etc

As you can see, the supporting needs are wide ranging – but they are worth investigating. Imagine 2 scenarios –

"Hi Mr Decision Maker. You should buy my product because it will help you make more profit!"

The decision maker will think – low research, not again, heard it before, you don't know my business etc….

Or

"Hi Mr Decision Maker. You should buy my product because it will help you control the shelf space and seasonal range concerns which I believe you have."

The decision maker will be more interested, he feels you have taken an interest, that you are trying to understand and that means he may ask for a few more details.

If we were to do a hierarchy of business needs, on a piece of paper for the hardware store visited in the show, I think it would look something like this –

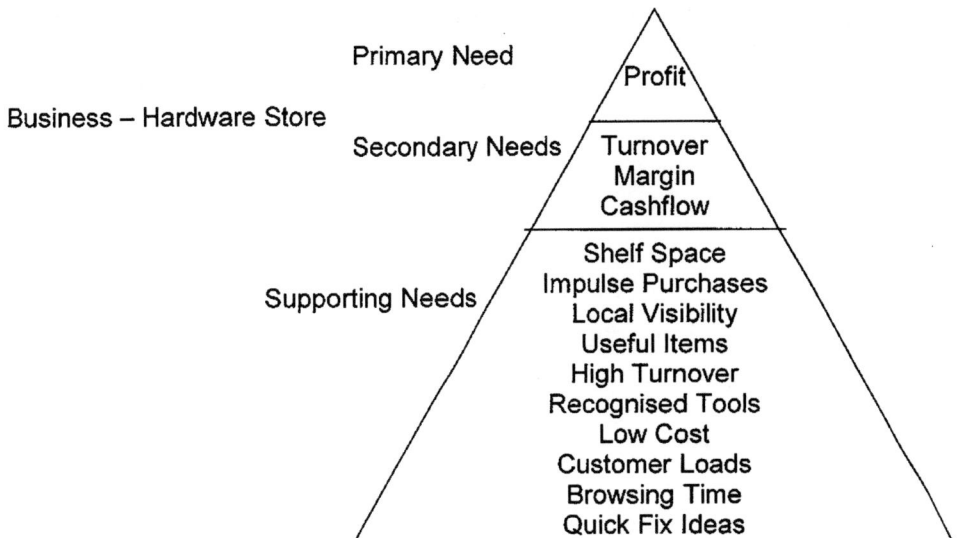

Which ones of these supporting needs are important? Most of them. Think about it. I've guessed these needs in a few minutes. Given some time I could come up with hundreds, but it is the spotting of the ones which are useful to you that matter. Heal's Hierarchy of Business Needs would be totally different, you'd see words like, style, time spent in store, imaginative gifts etc.

Let me take a few from the hardware store

- Shelf Space
- Impulse Purchase
- Useful Items
- High Turnover
- Low Cost
- Low Customer Load (What they have to carry)
- Quick fix ideas

Now, read those needs and tell me that they would not have

bought hundreds of the product which you used to stop the dust from drilling hitting your floor. These candidates were trying to sell them a sleeping bag!

Look at the words for Heal's

- Style
- High time spent in store
- Imaginative gifts
- Brand image
- Cool ideas

Now tell me that they would not have bought hundreds of the 'mojo' ball seat, or the tap coat hooks.

This, always in business is where to start. Identify your customer, figure out what they need and give it to them. The hierarchy of business needs is a perfect tool for this.

It proves the inadequacies of the candidates when Mona states – "I think this will be really easy to sell!" – TO WHOM?

These things really need some substance. All the products were good. In fact, the sleeping bag brought back some great memories. During the second world war, German tank commanders were issued with a similar thing for use on the Russian Front. It had no leg "items" as Howard describes them, but it did have arms, as well as a quick release zip which meant that you could pop your legs out quickly. My friend Toby and I got hold of one of these each when we were at Sandhurst and they were wonderful. On exercise, when the bad guys came, you could see Toby and I, still toasty in our sleeping bags, legging it down the hill with our legs out of the zip and the tail of the bag flapping behind us, whereas everyone else was fighting their way out of the mummy bags which were issued. Of course, everyone wanted one, but we had the only two. Imagine the success that sleeping bag would be in a camping shop outside the gates of any barracks, so long as it was green. There is a customer for every product, however this means that there is also a product for every customer and that is the place to start.

The other reason a focussed approach like this is good is because when you do then decide to set up some cold calls for the second day (these should be very much a bonus, not the main event) the calls can be focused. You are looking to make meetings in the same style of store and you can have this discussion on the phone, rather than phoning everyone in the yellow pages.

Pot luck is not good enough in the business world.

Then in this show came the pitch. I'll not depress all of us by speaking about it again at length – suffice to say, they were all as horrible and embarrassing as they usually are.

A couple of examples to help you in your business.

- The lady in the hardware store asks "How much does a normal sleeping bag cost?" Fair question. Howard has the great response of "Good Question" and Debra tells her that it can vary. Both of which are useless and wastes of breath. Know your market, know your nearest competitor.
- Howard asks – "Do you guys sell tents?" (I'll ignore the obvious disaster of calling a customer 'guys'). The answer was a simple "no". they should know this already. Research research research.

On a focused appointment or pitch like this you should expect orders in the hundreds. The very best the cold call appointments will ever give is the occasional order in the dozens. This is because, simply, you have a captive decision making audience with a warm lead, the cold leads will be fitting you in with who they have around. The best you will get is a trial period.

In business, use this knowledge. In The Apprentice, dive on it, it will save you from getting fired.

Finally, Mona managed to show me a good business lesson. If you give a concession, get one in return. She was asked, "Can you get the price down?" by the man in the camping shop. Her immediate reply was "can you increase the order?" Not bad. Although I would have been more forceful, "If you increase your order to X, I will decrease my price to Y". it keeps you in control. 5 out of 10 Mona, although James thought you were brilliant….

In short, your process should be –

- Look at your distributors, know their business
- Choose your product or products to pitch
- Show your knowledge in the pitch
- Negotiate an appropriately large order

It seems a good time now to take time to pen a word on attitude, knowledge and spotting body language.

A good friend of mine will only recruit people based on Attitude, Aptitude and Ability, in that order. His theory was proven on this show with the way Ben, Kate and Philip acted in their sub team. Their attitude was one of the reasons they failed. Philip's approach is always terrible, he shows this later in his demise in the boardroom.

On the subject of knowledge, Jasmina and Lorraine are discussing an order of 20,000 units. Lorraine had already asked the hardware store for an order of 5,000. This is clearly amateurish and ill prepared. In fact the hardware store man actually told her that it was not possible for him to sell that many, and she argued with him!! She knows nothing about his business and told him how many he could sell. Nonsense!

On spotting body language, a natural human skill, they went into Pets at Home and told two severely unimpressed ladies that were 'beaming with excitement'. We know these ladies are human because they got animated about another product earlier. This kind of thing just makes you look silly. When told that their product was targeted at boys, they should have said "yes it is!" Instead they babbled about boy and girl cats... they were then asked at whom the product was aimed and they again said – cats! Now, call me a fool, but I have never seen a cat with a wallet!

Know your customer, and theirs and also who the buyer will be – that is, the person who spends the cash! The were lucky to get an order for 50 – I suspect that was done to get rid of them.

In business, be aware of these three things, they are so important and can cause so much grief....

Having said that, I did have a warm glow inside watching Philip's performance, as I knew the whole way through that he was gone!

In summary. This task is all about research and understanding.

- Understand your distributor
- Choose your product with this in mind
- Pitch to the right level
- Negotiate large orders with knowledge and preparation

Boardroom Tactics

None needed this week. It was clear which team would win, it was clear who would be brought back in and it was very clear who would go!

Week Seven – the result!

Philip is wonderfully abusive to everyone.

Kate is actually quite good and the current favourite, however, she is showing some petulance and a bad attitude which could be dangerous. I assume she has been spoiled in the past.

Lorraine has factual sales on her side, but needs to stop playing the "instinct" card – it will not last much longer.

In the end – Philip, you're fired...... great choice Sir Alan. Nobody in their right mind would employ this fool.

Chapter Nine

"Jolly boy's outing?"

There is a reason that in the outstanding comedy "Only Fools and Horses", Del Boy and his pals went to Margate on their Jolly Boy's Outing. This is because that is what appealed to them. A while ago, for a certain type of consumer, Margate, Blackpool, Southport and all the other small seaside towns were appealing. They then lost their appeal slightly. With the influx of cheap package holidays abroad, all the people who went to the seaside towns were going away to Spain and Greece. The reduction in income resulted in a decline in appeal and the cycle continues. Recently, with more people realising the value of holidays and weekends in the beautiful country of Great Britain, for financial reasons as well as anything else, these towns have to grow into the 21st century – quickly.

This is why this task is an excellent one for the candidates. It's real life, it's relevant and above all, it's challenging. One of the most challenging tasks there is on the show in fact.

Sir Alan, as usual, tells the candidates this in the brief. He talks, with his usual red herring style, about rebranding the Millennium Dome where the analogy is clear. However, he also mentions the 'enterprising people' who rebranded the Dome and made a success of it. He also talks about the 'branding experts' to whom they will pitch. Herein lies the clue, Sir Alan is talking about consultancy and consultants and this is what the task is all about. Howard says almost immediately that the task is "all about rebranding" – it isn't. Sir Alan is looking for consulting skills in this task and all the candidates have again missed the point.

In the show, just as in business, consulting skills are vitally important. There is an old, and feeble, joke, but it works in this situation.

A real consultant is someone who borrows your watch and then charges you to tell you the time.

There is, as in all jokes feeble or otherwise, some truth in this. The art of consultancy is in helping the customer or client understand what they want or need and helping them do it. Remember the second line in the definition of selling "It begins with a discovery of needs to be met by the product being bought". What this means, in real terms is that most people don't know what they need until a skilled consultant brings out those needs during a business conversation. Always remember, it is better to be *interested* than *interesting*!

You will see that both teams set off on the same route – by identifying a target market. This is always the wrong place to start – go and do some research. Ask the people who matter, in this case the officials and locals of the town of Margate.

Step One – Research

Step Two – Target Market

Step Three – Design the Campaign

The only research done was by Mona, who comes from Kent and was not listened to (mainly as she has very little presence in the team). Mona and James went around and asked one or two people some questions, but as in many sales centred conversations, the questions they asked were focused on justifying the idea that they had already had. All the questions were around what people thought of the gay market – if you do research, take all your opinions away and ask people what markets THEY think will bring them in the profits they need. The market could be the gay market, or the family market, or the American, French, German or Hindu market – it does not matter until you have been told by the people that matter.

The main problem with trying to design a branding campaign on an idea based around no research is that you don't have what is known as evidential focus.

Evidential focus is when you give aspects of your campaign that run along the lines of –

We are giving you this because you/your people/the decision makers/the users told us that it is what was needed.

Without research, this does not work. With research, it works superbly. Mainly because it's the truth!

It is from these truths that slogans, photos, campaigns and leaflets come.

Clearly, as the candidates realised, it is far more fun to run around taking photographs or feeling important by interviewing candidates for a photo shoot. It happens in business all the time – it's called procrastination and stops you doing the job that you need to do.

Consulting, in essence is –

- Asking people open questions – the definition of an open question being one that makes people think – so you get the real truth!
- Finding out what they both want and need.

- Agreeing on a target market.
- Designing the rebranding campaign around the needs of the people.
- Pitch by telling the audience how you have designed a vision and concept around THEIR ideas (borrow their watch and charge them to tell them the time).

You'll notice the words I used there – vision and concept. Terrifyingly, I have found myself this week agreeing with Lorraine – mad as she is, she says that Sir Alan wants to see if they can differentiate between a concept and a product. She also says that poster is backed up by the leaflet and she's right on both counts.

Sadly though, the whole thing is useless without the pitch to the two different audiences. Again, some basic mistakes were made –

1 – There are two different audiences, pitch differently to them, tell people about your evidential focus and work to the audiences motivations

2 – Howard starts his pitch with a question but then does nothing with it. "Do you know Margate?" – So what?

3 – Never, ever lie, or fib, or bullshit or any euphemism for lying. "The leaflet is open for local adverts" IS A LIE – I would have immediately fired both Howard and Debra for this.

Finally on the pitch this week. If you are going to stand up in a suit and pitch (and believe me, sometimes you don't have to wear a suit) make sure you read the first part of this book about how you dress and look and then watch Howard on his pitch and you will see what I mean. Dark, ill fitting suit, black shirt and brown shoes, along with scruffy hair just looks awful. James is sitting down in the room looking far smarter, more professional and believable than Howard ever can.

In conclusion, consultancy is all about understanding people and giving them their needs in your own words. Try it on all areas of sales and you will see how it works.

Boardroom Tactics

All good things were said this week, most of which make a lot of sense. This task is usual for The Apprentice so listen to what Sir Alan says about posters, leaflets and pitches. He is a master at marketing both personally and business wise – otherwise he would not be the man on The Apprentice.....

People are now learning to keep their mouth shut in the boardroom, mainly because the loudmouth individuals, except Ben and Debra are gone.

The final three are an interesting bunch this week – James, Debra and Mona.

James is actually a good contender, although the best of a bad lot.

Debra is awful, horrid and a bully, but she will be fantastic television on the interview week, where she will be shown up.

Mona, is dull and quite useless.

Week Eight – the result!

Mona – you're fired. No other choice, well done again Sir Alan.

Chapter Ten

"Like taking candy....?"

Shows like the ones run at Earl's Court are famous for providers showing off their wares. They work, clearly, otherwise providers would not go to them and there are many modules of training around about how providers should act on these shows. How to dress, what to say to hook your prospect, what to offer and also the deals that you should think about giving. However, the real key to this is understanding how your customer thinks – let's face it, most people have been to a show like this, be it a wedding show, a pet show, a horse show, a car show or a baby show – the theory is the same. If you have been to one of these shows, by definition you will know how a customer thinks.

This is exactly why I was impressed at this week's episode when Lorraine announced that she had been to a baby show at Earl's Court. Kate jumped in with the first question that should be asked – "Why?"

In all sales, the question "Why?" is normally the first one that should be asked. Lorraine gave a great answer. She went there to look for furniture for her daughter's room. She also said that she remembers coming home with lots of 'impulse' purchases. What she means is that she went looking for ideas for her daughter's bedroom and saw things she had not thought of when she was there.

Let's be clear, there is no such thing that can be put simply into an 'impulse' purchase. People do not know what types of things are out there and how they can help. If an unusual, inexpensive and easy to transport product is on show, people will buy it – not because of impulse, but because at that moment they are clear on why they would use it. This is why petrol stations sell so many small gift items, when they are well displayed, they are an easy purchase, but you would have to be thinking about how they would be used when you buy them, or it would not happen. This takes 'impulse' away from it, as it can be managed by a great salesperson.

So, we need to start any task, or business project like this by thinking like a customer. When you are looking at the products to take on to a stand at a show, this is what you should be considering. You must have information and examples of the bigger sale items, but also many items that can be described, dealt with, paid for and taken away in moments. This will bring people to your stand and make you some initial money as well as giving people the information they need for the bigger items.

Some good questions were asked of the providers that the teams were seeing – have you done this before? Did you sell? – However, the crucial question of "How many did you sell ON THE DAY?" was continuously missed. I would bet that the birthing pool lady did not take £5,000 on a single day – for that to happen she would have had to sell 66 pools in a day – or 9 an hour. There is no chance of that happening. What she means (and she is not being dishonest, just answering the question that was asked) is that because of the day, she sold 66 pools – from orders, or people taking away information from the show. There is a huge difference and when your task is to sell ON THE DAY – the difference is key.

So, set your objective – if you want to sell things on the day, look for products that YOU would buy on the day, which would be cheap, easy to carry and simple to understand. The products that DON'T fall into this would be birthing pools (however practical) and rocking horses (however beautifully made). Sadly, the kind of products that DO fall into this category are travel prams, (everyone needs one and what could be easier to take away than a travel pram – it has wheels AND a carry bag!) baby crash helmets (oh please, I even hate wearing a helmet on my motorcycle – there's no way I'd put one of those on my child. However, I understand why people would buy them) and tragically, the high heeled shoes, no matter how vulgar, ugly and potentially degrading they are – I can imagine well meaning, but potty, aunts buying them in their hundreds......

The objective setting process would also drive some questions to ask yourself and the providers – for example –

- How much can I sell this for?
- Will people buy it TODAY?
- What is the competition for this product at the show?
- Is there room for negotiation or 'deals'?
- How many people will be at the show?
- How many times can I present this product in an hour?
- Can I present this product to a group?
- What will the split of customer types be? (In this case families of new parents/expectant mothers/new parents/single parents)

If you watch the rest of the episode this week, you will see how important each of these questions becomes.

Sales is all about questions – challenging both yourself AND your customer.

When the filing arrives at the show we immediately see Kate,

Lorraine and Howard realising that their product is already there – showing the importance of some of these questions.

My concern with both teams' approach was around the showing of the product – where was the planning and the approach – who decided it was better to talk to one person at a time and what was the reason for people to come to your stall – all these things need consideration.

Upon starting to sell at the show, there are a few rules.

- Remember the definition of selling
- Understand your 'elevator speech'
- Understand the 'cursors of power'

If we look again at the definition of selling we can see how this splits into three instructional areas with each sentence.

The best way to view selling is as a BUYING PROCESS which the salesperson brings about in the customer.

You must think about why people would be hooked to buy your pool / buggy / hat / horse or whatever your product is. What is your first question to a prospect? Do you present to a group or just one person? What part of your product will people like?

If the selling point of the buggy is how it folds, have a constant demonstration going on, the horse is beautiful, so people must touch and feel it, the hat is protective so get a dummy head and drop things on it, the pool is practical so have people try it out. Most of all, advertise these things are happening – constantly. Shout it out if you have to!

It begins with a discovery of needs to be met by the product being bought.

With a quick purchase you have to quickly identify, as well as having the customer identify, what the needs are.

- Who here has a child who is about to start to walk? – leads to the hat
- Who here has family based far away from them at the moment? – more people than a few years ago – leads to the pram
- Who here has anything beautiful to keep for their children and future generations? – leads to the horse
- Who here has done any research into home births? – leads to the pool

These are all questions, which immediately start the customer thinking – yes, my son is about to walk – so what? It is easy to get wrong, but even easier to get it dead right!

Secondly on this part is your own product knowledge – mixed with the motivations of the buyer (see previous chapters) which will bring it all together. Why would each of the 6 types of buyers motivation want your product. Get a reason for them to buy ready. James knows a little too much about the birthing pool and is coming across as an odd man in an odd suit with an odd fixation. Lorraine is useless at the basics of setting up her pram.

It should be enjoyable to both parties!

This is a baby show for heaven's sake! Even the men who are being dragged around by their partners are in a good mood as their proud parent side starts to come out. This is a perfect opportunity for some showmanship – present to a crowd, make people smile and get that product out there. Most of all, dress appropriately, nobody wants to see someone in a stuffy suit, particularly at Earl's Court where most people work in London all week and only ever see suits. It is meant to be fun, after all.

For those of you that don't know what an elevator speech

is – it is an American invention (otherwise it would be a 'lift speech') The principle is that if you got into a lift and realised your biggest prospect was in there with you and you had the time it takes to get to his or her floor to get a product pitch to them, what would you say?

Most people will claim that this never happens – which could be true. However, everyone must have an elevator speech. Why? Because many times in business we have to get the attention of a buyer straight away – on the phone, in a meeting or at a stand on a show.

There are two rules to an effective elevator speech. Both are completely strict, otherwise it will not work. There are, sadly, too many bad elevator speeches out there.

Rule one. Never, ever, ask a customer a question to which the answer could be no, because if you do, it will be.

Rule two. Set and be clear on your objective.

Rule one – why?

We are conditioned psychologically to answer no to salespeople. Try it out –

- Can I help you?
- Would you like to save money on your gas and electricity?
- Do you have a moment to talk?
- Would you like me to quote for fitted UPVC windows?
- Can I interest you in our birthing pool?
- Would you be interested in our birthing pool?
- Could I interest you in our birthing pool?

You'll notice that the last three were all asked, on this week's episode by Ben. Not surprisingly, the answers were and always will be, "NO!"

There are a group of people out there who tell young salespeople to ask these questions of prospects. They say that everyone would want to save money on gas and electricity etc. It's all wrong and needs to be stopped. If you asked one of these questions in an elevator and the answer was 'no' – it's a long old ride to that floor……

Think of a statement, not a question that will result in starting a conversation.

Hi, I'm Ben from Baby Boomer Birthing Pools Ltd. We know that only 2% of people consider home births – why do you think that is?

Once they have answered you say –

Interesting – one of the reasons is that people feel uncomfortable with the process at home – which is why we have designed this birthing pool – come and have a look for a moment!

End of elevator speech.

Rule two is just as important. Set your objective. For once, the objective here is NOT TO SELL. It is to get people to come and look. If you can identify my needs and give me all the features and benefits presentation in 30 seconds in a lift, I don't want your product because I could probably make it myself. Your objective here is to get someone to a stage where they will sit down with you and learn about your product. Therefore, an elevator speech needs a strapline and not a description of a product.

Finally, as was shown by James' team, last minute deals are always around. Sadly, they messed up this chance to win. Mainly because they had not asked the question around negotiating deals with people. A little gesture (although not Debra working for you for a week – I'd pay more for that not to happen…) would have resulted in a task winning sale here – I'm quite glad it didn't happen.

The cursors of power in business are important here. I remember a consultant talking to me on a flight on the way over to the US one time. He was off to see a large American Entertainment Imaging firm based in Rochester NY, to have a business meeting and was very nervous. He kept telling me how lucky he was to have come from a small company and have gained an opportunity to get such a big customer. He asked what I was doing and I said I was off to a similar meeting and I was pleased also, although for different reasons. My firm was around the same size as my travel companion and I was sure I was going to win the business – I did too, mainly because I understood the cursors of power. Who was the customer I was off to see? The same one as he…….

The cursors of power are something you should spend time on before any business negotiation or sale, no matter what size. People tend to concentrate on the first cursor (size) – which is open to some perception based fears – and ignore the others, however it is only when you put them together that you can validate the full picture.

They are as follows –

- The power of size   who is the bigger business?
- The power of choice   can they buy from anywhere else easily?
- The power of sanction   can you, or the person you deal with, stop the deal?
- The power of information   who knows most about the product, deal or issue?
- The power of time   when do they need this for, and when can you sell?

- The power of influence – can anyone influence your other dealings or contacts?

Clearly, the customer in this case had the power of choice – I can buy it now for £1,700 or later for £1,700. He also had the power of information – he knew where he could get it. The power of size, sanction and influence were equal, but the biggest problem was time – the customer knew that they needed to sell it NOW and so did the team – watch James and Ben's nervous faces…..

In this instance with three of the cursors equal and three on the side of the customer, there is no doubt what to do – DISCOUNT IT! However, they couldn't, because they had neglected a basic principle – ask the provider what they are allowed to sell it for…. This, and this alone, lost them the task and it was the fault of either Ben or Debra.

In summary, on a task like this.

- Think like a customer
- Set your objective
- Ask the provider, and yourself, the right questions
- Get your elevator speech ready
- Add some showmanship
- Understand the cursors of power

Boardroom Tactics

Sir Alan said it better than I could.

"Where was your reason for the man to buy today?" there wasn't one and as I said, that was the direct fault of either Ben or Debra. Sir Alan actually went (or sent someone, most likely) to the vendor and checked if they could discount, of course they could. So the final three line up was Ben, James and Debra.

Ben is again out of his depth – he is just spouting words which he has heard somewhere and has now lasted a week or so longer than I thought he would.

Debra is so awful that she will make excellent TV at the interview stage.

James, I think, has some brains, however, he is playing the comedy fop a little too much now.

Week Nine – the result!

Ben – you're fired! Thank you Sir Alan, good choice!

Chapter Eleven

"A real shot at TV stardom…?"

I was at school with a bloke who is now a shopping channel presenter. I can tell you from experience, there is certainly a distinct personality type who go for a job like that – I don't mean that in a bad way – this particular person was witty, articulate and clever and could hold the attention of a group for some time. Admittedly, after a while he did become annoying and repetitive, but you forgave him that for the odd moments of schoolboy comedy genius that emerged. I still chuckle at one or two of the things I remember him saying – particularly when the master's back was turned.

So, this week's task is an interesting one. Are we trying to succeed as a shopping channel presenter, or as a person of business – the two are very different. If you acted in business like you act on the channel – you would not last very long at all. Interesting to see that Debra did quite well on camera…

Let's take the successful shopping channel salesperson to start with and then move on to the business. There are two traits the successful shopping channel operative must have –

- Sales Skills
- TV Skills

The reason that they are on the shopping channel rather than 'Blue Peter' or 'Watchdog' is because their skills lie in between these areas – the same can be said for why they are not in business. The sales skills that are required here are all about speed of message, presenting a product with no idea who is tuning in, ensuring that the process is clear and sounding enthusiastic about, literally, anything that is being sold. The TV skills needed are the look, dress and image of a presenter, along with the ability to think on your feet, whilst taking direct instruction from the control booth and also, the ability to stop people switching off!

As far as The Apprentice is concerned – the one thing to remember is that this task ALWAYS comes up – it is one of Sir Alan's favourites – he finds it as funny as we do!

In this task, Sir Alan is looking for someone who can control a pitch under pressure – rather than someone who can present on TV. He needs fast decisions, reactions to the needs of the audience, clear instruction and knowledge of the state of sales.

The teams always, in this task, start to think about their target markets, what to buy, how to present the product and how to get their message across. All very important areas, however at this stage of the process, particularly if these are the brightest business talents in the country, they should be able to do that pretty quickly.

The link to business here is all about control of a sales campaign – the person in the control booth with the microphone link to the presenter is all – important. Like a conductor in an orchestra, the sales manager needs to carry the team forward, without that person, all will collapse. This is what Sir Alan knows and this is what he is looking for.

If you are a manager controlling a sales campaign, you need to know –

- The process the salespeople must follow
- What the salespeople should say
- When they should be saying it
- What the deal or reason to buy is
- How many of the product you have left to sell
- When they need to be sold by

Every day of a sales campaign, the sales manager should be pushing this to the sales people and this is clearly demonstrated in the world of TV shopping – the person in the booth is doing all these things over a short space of time. This means that the pressure is on and Sir Alan will be able to see how well it's done. Clearly, the results are in the sales and there are one or two factors which will add into the result, however, a good sales manager is the making of great salespeople.

Remember, as a sales manager, you need to manage your sales people to –

- Know what the key features of the product are
- Get the key messages across to customers
- Know how much stock you have left to sell
- Know how long they have left to sell it

Control is key and as a sales manager you need to be clear on every number at your disposal, and ensure the team knows these too – from an individual, team, organisation and industry point of view. Everyone needs targets and something to compete against; otherwise, they do not know how well they are doing. (For targets and competition, read – information to evaluate yourself and others, if you like….)

Ensure you constantly tell people –

- What to say to the customer

- What they look like to the customer
- What is important right now
- How others are doing
- How they are doing
- What their incentives are

Finally, make sure your information is correct. Debra hesitated when James and Jasmina were telling the wrong price to people – she should have jumped in straight away and rectified the mistake – I guarantee that this cost them some sales and if it had meant that they lost the task, Debra would have been out.

Some of the more simple actions in this task are worth noting briefly. As I wrote earlier, at this stage of the competition, the remaining candidates, irrespective of their earlier achievements, should have cottoned on to these actions – as should you in reading this book. If the remaining candidates have not yet grasped this, they are not long for the process.

Choosing the products.

The key points here are the same as in the previous task with the baby show. There are certain questions to be asked before you choose a product. For the show, a gamble on high price products could pay off – sell one or two and you have won, most people stick to the low priced volume products. The questions around products are listed below –

- Think of your target audience, people who buy from TV tend to fit into a certain type. Have you ever bought from TV (when sober)? If so, why? They tend to want ease of purchase, speed of purchase, economy purchases, gifts for friends (or enemies) and simple key messages.
- Think of how long you have to present the product. Can

you describe it in the time? What are the key selling points? Can you bring it to life?
- Can you demonstrate it? how much room does it need? Does demonstrating it make it a good offer?

Choosing your presenters.

The next part of this task was choosing who would present alone and who would do it in a team – if you are deciding a similar split with your teams, ensure that the strongest presenters are tasked to their strengths and people who need someone to lean on are put together. If you are on the show itself and doing this task, my advice would be –

- Listen to the experts. The people on the channel do this day in and day out, they know what to look for and who has it. Use them.
- Think about the image. Howard's continually unbuttoned collar irritates me when I'm just watching the show, never mind considering buying from him and the fact that he does not seem to own a shirt that is not black, red or brown worries me. I would buy nothing from him, face to face or on television. I have said it before, if you are wearing a suit, wear it like a suit. If you want to be trendy, put some jeans on. Polarising people with your dress code is a wrong turn.
- Agree on control instructions from the booth – if the presenter is not clear on what you want them to do, they will not follow you. For an example of this see Jasmina being told 10 times to shut up and let James state the price of the product.
- Think about how to stop people turning off. What is the constant message? Who has the best camera presence? Why do people watch in the first place?

Finally, the main thing with this type of sale is to get the real messages across quickly and efficiently. It is not as easy as it seems – remember when you watch these shows, the presenters may seem like odd, quirky or irritating, but they are the professionals.

- Tell your audience what the product is
- Tell them why they should buy it
- Tell them how much it is
- Tell them how to buy it

Speak slowly and clearly and most of all – be ENTHUSIASTIC!

Boardroom Tactics

The boardroom is becoming more interesting now – Sir Alan knows that most of the rubbish is cleared and he is keeping some good television characters in for the final run in. I see Kate and one other (probably James) in the final, for the others, it is just a case of who would be most fun in the interview task – we all know who that will be.

The final three in the boardroom this week were a diverse bunch.

Lorraine is not a quick thinker, but will be fun in the interviews. This task needed quick thinking so really, she should have been on a loose brick.

Howard is very dull and is totally the opposite of the 'flair' that Sir Alan is looking for.

Kate showed enthusiasm in this task and has had some flashes of talent in the show – she'll do well, although it seems she becomes petulant under what she sees as criticism, which is a childish trait.

Week Ten – the result!

Howard – you're fired! The right choice again, he is far too dull for this great show.

Chapter Twelve

"Interview, or interrogation?"

It is important to note that whilst this task appears in every series of the show, it is NOT about interview techniques. What these candidates go through is not a "rigorous interview process". It is more of an interrogation.

If it was an interview, it would happen at the start of the process, with proper processes in place for the interviews. An interview is designed so the interviewer can gauge the interviewee's competency for a job, and to give the (probably nervous) interviewee the best chance of showing off their skills – otherwise it is a pointless exercise.

What we have here is reality TV at it's best. This makes wonderful TV, a group of people interrogating some over inflated egos and bringing them down a few pegs. It is fantastic fun – I'd love to be on the panel myself!

The best part about it is that the candidates approach it like an interview (even if it were an interview they would still be showing poor skills) and get pulled to pieces. Lorraine states at the start that she is "very, very good at interviews." This was a very bad place to start.

This chapter, more than all the others needs to be split into two. If you want to be part of the show, we need to discuss the tactics in the interrogation. If you want to be more successful in your interviews, we need to look at that separately.

The TV interrogation

Let's start with the protagonists, the "interviewing" panel that Sir Alan chooses. Why do these people get to interview the candidates?

Firstly, it makes good TV. Here we have 4 confident, aggressive, smart, successful people, but most of all Sir Alan trusts them. If you watch the show, you will seldom see them agreeing on a person when discussing them in the boardroom. This is a good thing, it makes even better TV. It also proves that the panel is not interviewing, because they are all different types of people who are tasked with looking for a different type of person. This also proves a second point – even though Sir Alan trusts them and knows they will do him a good job, the fact that they disagree points to them not helping his decision making.

Sir Alan has already made up his mind who he will fire this week. We all know that he would never give Debra a job. She is in this episode because of the on screen value she has in these situations.

Therefore the way to approach this is that your fate is already sealed and if it is positive, you should prove your worth and if it is negative, it is your last chance to really shine, it may save you.

If we take a look at some of the mistakes the candidates made in this episode, both on interrogation and interview techniques, it will bring the conclusions together.

James

- Used jargon in his application – nobody knows what a 'rate busting NGM' is!
- Got sent into a frenzy by everyone and is easily flustered

Kate

- Should have been more ready for the 2 obvious questions
    - "Tell me something about yourself"
    - "What are you doing here?"

Jasmina

- If you claim to be an FD – make sure you know your numbers and the basic terminology
- Did not come across as credible

Lorraine

- Got very flustered and confused
- Was not honest on her application

Debra

- Being unpopular is nothing to be proud of, and only acceptable if you can absolutely defend it

There are some standard errors that always come up on this particular episode, avoidance of these errors is one way to ensure that the attack you are about to get is reduced, or even held off – the winner last year had Claude speechless and another interviewer beaming when he reeled off his knowledge of Sir Alan. He, from then, was unstoppable.

The reason that these standard errors come up is because the candidates, when preparing, are not applying for a job, but a place on a reality show. This promotes boasting on a CV, outrageous statements on application forms and mis-spent preparation time – however, without these, you may not get on the show in the first place…..

For this episode, ensure that –

- You know Sir Alan *inside out*. People on this show seldom do their research, you need to know the man, the business and the values without question. This one thing will get you out of any attack from his cohorts
- Do not rise to the attacks on interrogation. Pause before each answer and think about your body language and what you are about to say. They will prey on your ego, pummelling it until you break – keep it together
- These people will know *everything* about you. Be prepared to justify any skeletons and don't be surprised at their knowledge
- Be polite. Don't show a blasé approach or any bad attitude
- Look smart. No outrageous clothing. This is business, not fun
- Show them your passion and that you want the job

Do these things and the likelihood is that you will emerge unscathed – although if Sir Alan has already decided that your time is up – you'll be fired whatever you do.

Proper interviews

We should start with a CV, that is where most interviews start after all. A CV, curriculum vitae or resume is a précis of your professional life thus far. It should never cover more than 2 pages, should never be in a bright colour (one thing that will guarantee you not to have an interview) and should be set out professionally.

The CV should cover your career roles and the achievements thereof. You should spend a lot of time telling the reader what you had to do and what the result was – all in the third person. Finally, there should be a small amount of personal information on there, just to bring you to life.

The interview need not dwell too much on the CV. If it has done it's job, you should be at the stage where people are asking you what you are going to do for them, not what you have done in the past for others…

Most interviews these days take the form of a competency based interview. Normally I detest the word competency, because it smacks of average, or normal standards and we should all strive to be the best. However, in this case it works well as a word because the idea is that the interviewer is looking to see if the interviewee can PROVE competence by EXPERIENCE and KNOWEDGE for them to be able to perform adequately at the job on offer. Competency based interviews (CBI) are seldom done correctly, as the role of an interviewer in these situations is to pull relevant information from a subject, and as all good salespeople know, this is quite hard to do – therefore people don't do them properly.

The good thing about a CBI is the simplicity of preparation and implementation. There is much to be gained from an internet search on 'competency based interviews', most of which is summarised below.

When invited for a competency based interview, firstly ask the interviewer which competencies will be focused on for the role – they should tell you. From this you can work out what the questions will be. For example, if the competency is "Customer Service" and the description of this competency is that one "must show the ability to retain a great customer even when under competitive pressure" – it is a fair bet to say that the question on that competency will be – "tell me when you have retained a great customer even when under competitive pressure".

See how they work? The competency is split into a description and the question is always leading you to give them an example of when you have done it – or if you have never done it, what you would do in that situation.

So, if you get a list of competencies and descriptions, a simple internet search will provide sample questions that an interviewer would ask to display these competencies. Get a close friend who is direct on feedback to role play it with you.

Interviewer should tell you what the competency is that they are testing and the description – this helps you form your answer around it – remember, they are not there to challenge you, but to give you the best chance of showing your worth. If you are not clear on what they are testing, or what the question is – ask – I would rather employ someone who was confident enough to ask than a bluffer.

When answering, follow the simple process of P-STAR.

Pause!

Situation

Task

Action

Result

The pause helps you remember your preparation, if done properly, you should have already asked yourself this question and got an answer ready.

Situation – give the interviewer a *brief* description of the situation you found yourself in which best describes the competency

Task – because of the situation, this is what I had to do

Action – so this is what I actually did

Result – and this is what happened because of what I did

Nice and simple – it stops waffling and bluffing and also helps you know that you have covered your answer sensibly. Remember – the RESULT is normally all important. If you did everything right, but still lost a great customer, then it's a bad example! Finally, the examples do not always have to be business linked. The odd sporting simile or club example is great to show you are a well rounded individual who does not just work and watch television.

A final tip – when asked "Have you got any questions for us?" don't drop into the trap of asking about salary, holidays and those areas – nor should you just mumble "no". show an interest in the business – who knows what keeps the interviewer working there, for example.....

In summary, if you are going on the show, get yourself ready for a grilling for the sake of TV. Know Sir Alan and justify your skeletons, other than that, I can't help.

If you are going for an interview – prepare! We have all heard of the 7 P process (proper preparation and planning prevents p*ss poor performance), and there is no greater example of it than this. It is easy to prepare for a CBI, so do it and answer all the questions with a P-STAR!

Boardroom Tactics

None needed this week – Sir Alan had his fun. Ensure if you

are in this position that you have any justification for mistakes ready. You'll know the ones you made, think about your last chance at staying in.

He was always going to fire 3 people – the final has to be between two. I thought I knew who the final 2 were and was surprised at one of them.

Kate seems steady and smart, with some petulant traits

Jasmina let herself down over the accounts, but has been good in some project manager roles

Lorraine is looking quite dim now and is relying too much on 'intuition'

Debra is just an awful bully

James is showing equal flashes of genius and folly

Week Eleven – the result!
Well, the first time Sir Alan and I have disagreed.

I thought it was sure to be a James and Kate final – at least I was half right. In fact, I actually thought James would be the overall winner, but then, he chose the comedy act last year in Simon.

Therefore, it is to be a final between Kate and Jasmina. Roll on next week!

Chapter Thirteen

"A worthy winner?"

The final has arrived. Kate and Jasmina go head to head on a task, helped by their previously fired peers, for the crown of Sir Alan's apprentice 2009.

Clearly, all business lesson, from both reading this book, watching the show and being on the show should be well implemented by now. Therefore let's have a look at why Jasmina, rather than Kate, walked away with the first prize.

The task was all about building a new brand of chocolates and the teams started well. The ideas brought out were clever – a chocolate box for couples and a chocolate box (initially) for men. These ideas are new, off the wall and creative, so there is no doubt that both these young women have either a creative streak, or the ability to bring that streak out in others.

A very impressive occurrence was when Jasmina decided to drop her idea of the all male chocolates and change tack – this shows that she can take feedback, and make a decision – that is important.

However, Kate's idea was superior – she had a target audience, a good set of flavours and a good plan for her team. Nick Hewer even commented on this, saying "All they need now is a name".

Kate went about this the right way, she sat down and created a brand and a name around and idea. Jasmina, on the other hand, created an idea and brand around a name.

The product launches were good, creative and to the point, although, both presentations were very disappointing – as is normally the case on this show. Kate came across as stilted and therefore unbelievable, Jasmina was too animated on some points. She pauses for applause, which never comes, which shows a lack of planning.

Kate is vague on the questions she is asked – people think the flavours are good and then ask about profit – she tells them there is 'enough' for everyone. Jasmina is very clear on the profit, telling us it costs a mere 7 pence per chocolate to make. However she starts the main part of her presentation with "the important question of price", which is the wrong place for it.

When all was over – it was undoubted that Kate's idea was better, her brand was better and her chocolates certainly tasted better – Jasmina goes for cheaper ingredients and money saving and ends up with a worse package all round – so, why did Jasmina end up winning?

The answer is somewhat simple – in this case, she was just what Sir Alan wanted and – vital to him – what he understood. She is entrepreneurial, risk taking and focused, just like him.

She has good decision making skills – shown when she changes her planned target audience.

She has passion, shown when in the spotlight on many occasions and in her interrogations last week.

She can manage people well – shown in the restaurant task.

She has clarity of thought, which means she can learn and be moulded by Sir Alan.

These are all reasons why she was chosen over Kate.

However, most important, there is one thing that clinched it, and, luckily for me, it proves a theory I discussed earlier in this book.

There are only 6 reasons why people buy.

- That they can trust the product or the business involved (Safety)
- That they love the brand and wish to be associated with it (Honour)
- That they enjoy the research and development, or innovation of the product or business (Advancement)
- That they feel they are looked after when the deal is done (Protection)
- That they are getting value for money (Economy)
- That they know and trust the people involved (Relationship)

These are easily remembered by the mnemonic SHAPER©. Remember, people's buying motivations NEVER change, it is inbred in our psychology and you will only recognise up to three of them. This is why people sometimes don't understand why people spend money. If you understand this, you can sell to anyone.

Most people however, will only recognise those who share their motivations. How many times have you said that you can deal with one person and you don't seem to be able to deal with another…look closely at their buying motivations and you'll see why. You can identify a person's buying motivations with clever questioning, but if you want to go into that, read my next book!

Jasmina and Sir Alan share one buying motivation, that

of Economy. It is very strong in both of them, shown by his constant focus on profit and her constant drive to lower the price of product suppliers – sometimes to the detriment of the product developed. This trait is also quite important in the current climate.

Furthermore, neither of them worry too much about Safety or Protection.

This does not mean that you will only win if you follow Sir Alan's buying motivations (Economy, Advancement and Honour, in that order, if you're interested), but it does mean that Kate and Jasmina were so close at the end that he went with what he knows and what he is comfortable with – like so many people in business.

Boardroom Tactics

The only tactic in this boardroom is to have, completely prepared, your closing statements to Sir Alan. These should revolve around your potential for his business, what (specifically) you have done well in the show and how you can learn and develop under him. The main thing is – be brief, clear and well thought out. Now is not the time for postulation.

Week Eleven – the result!

Jasmina – you're hired!!! Well done, a good victory and probably the right choice right now in the current climate. She'll save Sir Alan money and provide a good management service, however, she may compromise the quality of goods sold – it is fair to say that after seeing her approach in this series, I would not be rushing to go to her restaurant....

Commiserations to Kate, I knew she would do well and actually thought she had won it with her excellent chocolates and brand. Bad luck, but I'm sure she will do well in the future.

Chapter Fourteen

"So what?"

The title of this final chapter is probably the most important question anyone in business can ever ask themselves. When you look at the feature of a product, ask it. when you tell a customer, or a client about your product, ask it. When you look at a target audience, or a new brand, ask it. Therefore, we should ask it as the final question in this book.

So what? What have we decided on the subject of "How to Survive The Apprentice". The show this year was as excellent as ever. We were stunned and saddened at the end by the departure of Margaret, but I'm sure that Sir Alan will find a competent replacement. We watched in horror as Kate and Philip got together and covered our ears whenever Ben mentioned Sandhurst. We laughed at Lorraine and shuddered at Debra. Noorul bored us and James confused us. All the major elements of fun were there.

Aside from that, we can be sure that there have been some major business lessons, I'd like you to remember something from each chapter.

1. Dress for business
2. Think of the objective of your task
3. Ensure you know your pricing and defend it

4. There is a cycle to the sales process
5. There are 5 distinct steps to negotiation
6. Research and understanding makes the process clearer
7. Consultative selling is a key skill
8. Presenting to your audience should be straightforward
9. Hierarchy of business needs
10. Elevator Speeches and the cursors of power
11. Get your message across
12. P-STAR for interviews
13. Make sure the person to whom you are selling knows why they should buy from you!
14. Business is full of lessons – watch out for them and take everyone's opinion for what it is – an opinion. Watching and learning can overtake any obstacle

The most important thing, and if you only take one thing away from this book, let it be this:

Francis Bacon once said –

"Half of wisdom is a great question."

Good questions are at the heart of all business and the heart of business is selling. Write down the definition of selling and look at it every time you visit a customer – it, more than anything else will improve your business skills tremendously.

The best way to view selling is as a buying process which the salesperson brings about in the customer.

It begins with a discovery of needs to be met by the product being bought.

It should be enjoyable to both parties.

Thank you, and good luck.

Matthew R Quinn

Acknowledgements

This book would not be possible without the following people – whether they knew it or not.

My Mum, for giving me the love of the English language and the longing to write. My Dad, for giving me the same love of business. My best pal, Proccy, for scathingly claiming I'd never do it, so laying down a challenge. My mucker Toby, for making me want to do something when he was away overseas doing a job he loves that is far more important than mine. Andy Paterson, friend and ex colleague, for many nights overseas on jobs or bike trips, working out all the processes on a beer mat. My boss, Peter, for constantly challenging me for ideas, whilst also making me laugh at the world in general. My old school for inviting me back to speak at the prize giving evening and so making me do something worth speaking about. Most of all and finally, my beautiful and supportive wife Wendy, who never thinks anything I do is silly, even though most of it is.

About the Author

Matthew Quinn was born and brought up in Oldham Lancashire before attending the Royal Military Academy at Sandhurst. He left the Army in the mid nineties and began his civilian life in the motor trade. After deciding that he had reached his peak as business manager in the flagship Mercedes Benz dealership in London's Park Lane at the age of 27, Matthew went on to be a senior consultant for one of Europe's largest management consultancies. For 5 years he travelled extensively around the world selling, designing and delivering high impact sales and sales management programmes for many businesses, most notably in the oil, entertainment and fast moving consumer goods industries.

Matthew currently works as head of business development for a major financial services firm and draws on the lessons learned in all the sales areas in which he has worked, as well as leadership and management lessons learned in the forces.

Matthew lives with his wife Wendy, just outside Edinburgh and enjoys powerboating, fishing, shooting, cooking, camping, walking, travel, scuba diving, motorcycling and running. He says a person cannot have too many hobbies. Matthew is also proud to be an ambassador for the John Thornton Young Achiever's Foundation.

This is his first book.

Lightning Source UK Ltd.
Milton Keynes UK
21 November 2009

146539UK00002B/1/P